OUR CATHOLIC FAMILY

Activities, Conversations, and Prayer
for Sharing Faith at Home

David Dziena and Gloria Shahin

Interior design and typesetting by Victory Productions, Inc.

All interior photos ©Thinkstock:

pp. 8-9 Digital Vision
pp.14-15 Pavel Losevsky
pp. 28-29 monkeybusinessimages
pp. 48-49 Andreas Rodriguez
pp. 66-67 Comstock
pp. 78-79 monkeybusinessimages
pp. 90-91 Creatas Images
p. 97 Design Pics

Pflaum Publishing Group
A division of Bayard, Inc.
2621 Dryden Road, Suite 300
Dayton, OH 45439

ISBN 978-939105-4315-1

HTP-4315-M

WELCOME!

We all have this natural desire for the sacred in our lives. We all want unconditional love. We all want to belong to something or someone bigger than ourselves. We all want to say yes to God as our Father, and yes to Jesus as our Brother and Savior. This natural longing for the sacred is the journey of our lives. If we listen to the Holy Spirit, all our roads lead to God.

But sometimes things can get in the way. We get busy. We get distracted. We let the seasons of the Church year (and even the seasons of the natural year, the dying of autumn and winter, the emerging life of spring and summer, illustrating the great lesson of the Church year, the dying and rising of Christ) pass by without notice. We forget that, in the Church year, every season is a season of grace. Every day is a saint's day. Surely we can find the time to celebrate at least some of them.

This book will help you to do that. There is nothing complicated here. Mainly, it is a book of "look and see." Look at what you can see in the seasons of the Church year and in the world around you, and share it with your family in a simple and straightforward way. Look at the riches of the liturgy of the Church, and make it your own, in your own way, in your own household, in your own "domestic church." These riches are yours. This book can help you to recognize them. Take them, use them, and help your family to grow in faith and in love.

Jesus invites us to meet him by seeing where he lives. Jesus, the Risen One, lives among us in the here and now, in the loving chaos of family life. As he invites us to share his table at the Eucharist, let us invite him to share ours at home, as we celebrate a year of grace with him.

TABLE OF CONTENTS

PART 1: BRINGING THE LITURGY HOME

"Parents have shared the gift of human life with their children and, through Baptism, they have enriched them with a share in God's own life."

(National Directory for Catechesis, p. 203)

The Sunday and Daily Readings

The Mass readings for each day of the week can be found online, at the Website of the United States Conference of Catholic Bishops. Enter www.usccb.org/bible/readings into your search engine, or search for "daily readings" and this website will be among the ones offered. You may want to read the Sunday Gospel aloud at supper on Saturday night, just to familiarize your family with it. Or, you may want to read it for yourself, just to be a step ahead of them during Sunday's car talk!

Throughout this resource, if a feast should fall on a Sunday, you will not find the readings on the USCCB website. The Sunday readings usually take precedence over a feast day (with the exception of the greater feasts of Our Lord). To find the readings for the saint, you may want to search online for "Readings for the Proper of the Saints" or "Readings for Other Masses" (which includes the Common of the Saints). You will find the citations for the readings there, and you can look them up in your Bible.

Before-Mass Car Talk
Use the time in the car before Mass to "prime the pump" so that the family will have something to look for or listen for in the Sunday Mass.

The following questions may help. They do not all apply to every Mass, but are general questions which can help children to get ready to understand something from the Mass, to learn something from the homily, to participate in some way with more attention.

- What season of the year are we in? *(spring, summer, fall, winter)*

- What season of the Church year are we in? *(Advent, Christmas, Lent, Easter, Ordinary Time)*

- What color vestment do you think the priest will be wearing? Why? *(See the note on "Liturgical Colors" at the end of this section.)*

- What decorations are in the church? Do you remember seeing any last Sunday?

- What is your favorite stained-glass window in church? *(Occasionally take time after Mass, preferably a few times a year, to look at the windows and the statues, so that your child becomes familiar with them and with the stories behind them. The Christmas Crib should be visited on Christmas Day and on each Sunday of the Christmas Season. The statues are almost life-sized, and a child can easily place himself or herself in the stable.)*

- Who knows what we say when the priest says, "Lord, have mercy"? What does he say next? What do we say back?

[Quiz other Mass responses as well: the responses at the Preface, ("The Lord be with you." "And with your spirit." "Lift up your hearts." "We have lifted them up to the Lord.") or the Amen after "Through him, with him, in him," when the priest holds up the large Host.]

- What reading is the Gospel reading? *(the one we stand up for)*

- Why do we stand up? *(because it is about Jesus, the Son of God)*

- What do you think Jesus will say or do in the Gospel today? Will he heal someone? Will he tell a story? Will he tell us how to live better? What do you think he will do today? What will he say to us today? Let's listen hard and check back after Mass!

After-Mass Car Talk

- What color were the priest's vestments today?

- What season of the Church year are we in?

- What story did Jesus tell in the Gospel? (or) What was the Gospel about today?

- What Gospel writer did we hear from today? *(Matthew, Mark, Luke, or John)*

- What did Jesus say (or do) in the Gospel today?

- What joke did Father tell during the homily? What story did Father tell during the homily?

- Let's all think of one thing Father said about the readings.

- Let's all think of one thing Father suggested that we do to follow Jesus better.

- How can our family be better followers of Jesus?

- Who did you shake hands with at the Sign of Peace?

- [If Communion was received] Did you remember to thank Jesus for coming to you in Holy Communion? Did you tell Jesus anything special today?

- We all feel good about going to Mass. We know God loves us and cares about us, and we have received Jesus himself in Holy Communion. How are we going to share God's love with one another? How are we going to share God's love outside of our own family?

More about the Mass

Children's Mass Books

Look online in a local Catholic bookstore for Mass Books for children. Find one that matches your child's age and reading ability. Look for colorful, child-friendly art. At Mass, help your child match the book page to what is happening now. These books are valuable learning tools that can be read both at home and in church.

Liturgical Colors
The following are the meanings of the liturgical colors used in the Church's liturgy:

Green – Ordinary Time

Violet – Advent and Lent

Rose – Gaudete Sunday (Third Sunday of Advent) and Laetare Sunday (Fourth Sunday of Lent)

Red – Palm Sunday, Good Friday, Pentecost; Feasts of Martyrs, Apostles, and Evangelists; the Sacrament of Confirmation

White – Christmas and the Christmas Season; Holy Thursday; the Easter Season; Feasts of Our Lady; Feasts of saints who were not martyrs; Feasts of Our Lord which do not recall his Passion (Christ the King, Corpus Christi)

Ranks of Liturgical Feast Days
Each day of the year has a designated celebration. The most important days are called Solemnities. These have the highest rank. The next in rank are Feasts, usually of major events in the life of Jesus or Mary, or the days of major saints in the Church. The next in rank are Memorials. These memorials are usually of saints celebrated by the entire Church. *Optional memorials* are memorials that commemorate a less well-known saint or a saint associated with a particular country.

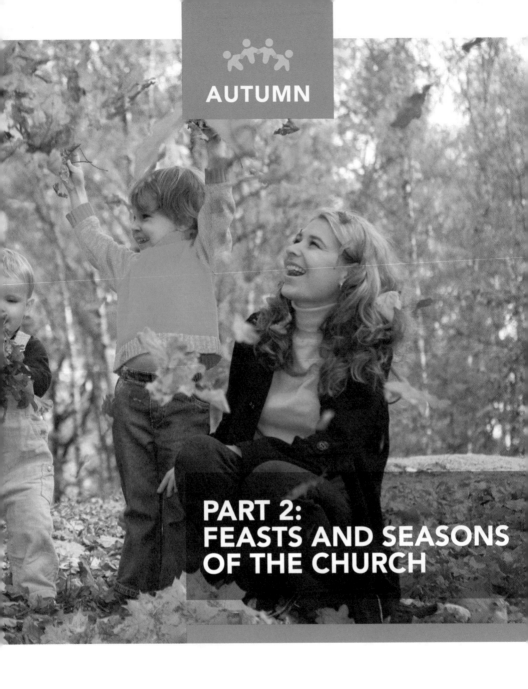

AUTUMN

**PART 2:
FEASTS AND SEASONS
OF THE CHURCH**

Then let all of the trees of the forest
rejoice before the LORD who comes,
who comes to govern the earth,
To govern the world with justice
and the peoples with faithfulness.

(Psalm 96:12–13, NABRE)

September

Although many school years begin in August, the month of September still signals the end of one season and the beginning of another. Summer is ending, yet there are still a few days warm enough to spend outdoors. Be sure to set aside time on the weekends to enjoy them with family and friends!

The flower designated for this month is the aster, from the Greek word for star. It symbolizes love, faith, and wisdom. Take a family walk through your neighborhood and see how many asters you can find! They come in the colors of pink, red, white, lilac, and mauve.

September is a transitional time, especially for children, who are getting used to new routines, new teachers, and perhaps new friends. Be alert to give encouragement and reassurance as needed. Children do want to grow up, but that does not mean that it is always easy!

The blessings and prayers below are offered as helps during this transition time. You may want to tuck a favorite one into your child's daily planner for use during a quiet moment at school.

 ### Prayers for a New School Year
A Parent's Blessing for the First Day of School
A reading from the Book of Proverbs:
"Happy the one who finds wisdom,
    the one who gains understanding!
Her profit is better than profit in silver,
    and better than gold is her revenue. . . .
Her ways are pleasant ways,
    and all her paths are peace."
(Proverbs 3:13–14, 17)

God of Wisdom,
As we begin a new school year, we ask you to be with our child (children). Help her (him) to listen, to participate, to help others, and to make good friends in school. Help her (him) to find and use the gifts and talents you have given, and to share your love with others. We ask this in the name of your Son, Jesus Christ.
All: Amen.

Put your hand on your child's head and, with your thumb, trace the Sign of the Cross on your child's forehead.

And now I bless you, *[name]*, in the name of the Father, and of the Son, and of the Holy Spirit. Amen. May all your paths be peace!

Daily Prayers and Blessings to Start the School Day
An Irish Blessing
May the road rise to meet you.
May the wind be ever at your back.
And may the Lord hold you
in the hollow of his hand.

A Prayer to the Holy Spirit
Holy Spirit of God, be with me. Fill my heart with your love.
Help me show kindness to others. Bring me wisdom and joy today.
Amen.

Pope Francis's Prayer to the Holy Spirit
Holy Spirit, may my heart be open to the Word of God, may my
heart be open to good, may my heart be open to the beauty of
God, every day.
Amen.

 Feast of the Nativity of the Blessed Virgin Mary
(September 8)

Introduction

*Because the Church has designated December 8 as the feast of Mary's
Immaculate Conception, the date of September 8 is chosen as her birthday
celebration. Celebrate Mary's birthday in honor of her special place in the life
of Jesus, and in the life of all humanity: "Of her was born Jesus who is called
the Christ" (Matthew 1:16).*

*As a family, complete all of the following faith-sharing steps, or do one or
more as time permits.*

Today's Reading

Go to www.usccb.org/bible/readings for the text or an audio recording of the
Scripture readings for the Feast of the Nativity of the Blessed Virgin Mary. Note that
there are two choices for each of the readings (the first reading and the Gospel).

Faith-Sharing Activity

Nothing says "birthday" like cupcakes and candles! Invite the family to make cupcakes together, with a boxed mix or your favorite recipe. Using food coloring, dye
white frosting blue (Mary's color) and frost the cupcakes. Put a birthday candle
in each one, so each family member can blow out a candle. Don't forget to sing
"Happy Birthday" first!

Conversation Starter

We don't know how the Holy Family celebrated birthdays, but we do know that Mary and Joseph were good parents. How do we know? *(They took care of Jesus. They looked for him when he was lost.)*

Today's Prayer

Dear God,
As we celebrate Mary's birthday, we thank you for giving her to us as the Mother of God and our Mother, too. We ask her to bless our family and to always be with us. We ask this through her Son and yours, Jesus Christ, our Savior.
Amen.

(Conclude by praying a "Hail, Mary" together.)

Feast of the Exaltation of the Holy Cross (September 14)

Introduction

The Feast of the Holy Cross has been celebrated by the Church since the fourth century. It originally commemorated the dedication of the Church of the Holy Sepulcher in Jerusalem in 335 A.D. On September 14, a portion of the True Cross (found by Saint Helena in 326) was brought inside this church for veneration.

Today's Reading

Go to www.usccb.org/bible/readings for the text or an audio recording of the Scripture readings for the Feast of the Exaltation of the Holy Cross.

Faith-Sharing Activity

Today's feast is joyful and triumphant, a victory celebration. In that spirit, form a "victory procession" through your house. Carry a crucifix from the front door into each room. In each room, pray the following designated prayers. (The response is: Because by your holy Cross you have redeemed the world.)

Living Room: Lord Jesus, bless this room where we receive our family and friends as welcome guests. We adore you, O Christ, and we bless you. *(All respond.)*

Dining Room: Lord Jesus, bless this room where we share our meals, especially with guests. We adore you, O Christ, and we bless you. *(All respond.)*

Kitchen: Lord Jesus, bless this room where we prepare our meals and gather as a family. We adore you, O Christ, and we bless you. *(All respond.)*

Family Room: Lord Jesus, bless this room where we gather for fun, recreation, and family sharing. We adore you, O Christ, and we bless you. *(All respond.)*

Each bedroom: Lord Jesus, bless this room where (name) sleeps. In rest, may he (she) find healing and peace in body and soul. We adore you, O Christ, and we bless you.

(All respond.)

Conversation Starter
Jesus' Cross is a sign. A sign tells you something. What does the Cross tell you? Jesus died because some people did not like his message. What was his message?

Today's Prayer
Thank you, Jesus, for giving us the Cross as a sign of your victory. Help us to remember that you are with us always, especially in the Eucharist.
Amen.

(Make the Sign of the Cross together.)

 # October

During the month of October, autumn comes into its own. All around us, the world prepares for winter. In many parts of our country, squirrels are busy hiding nuts. Snow shovels and snow blowers appear in hardware stores. We are urged to winterize our automobiles before it is too late and we are caught with a dead battery or worse.

But in the Church year, October brings special feasts and celebrations: Our Lady of the Rosary, Saint Thérèse of Lisieux, the great Saint Francis of Assisi, and the feast days of two beloved popes, Saint John XXIII and Saint John Paul II. And how could we forget All Hallows' Eve (Halloween)?

The flower for the month of October is the marigold (thought to be named for Our Lady, "Mary's Gold"). In "flower-language" it symbolizes sorrow or sympathy, but its cheerful and sturdy blossoms also remind us of the compatibility of strength and beauty in our lives. How much do we need that balance!

 ## Memorial of Saint Thérèse of the Child Jesus (October 1)

Introduction
As a fifteen-year-old, Saint Thérèse was allowed to enter the Carmelite monastery of Lisieux, France, and was thought to be living a simple but obscure life. It was only after her death that her "little way of spiritual childhood"—doing little things out of great love—became known and accessible to the world. Not all of us have great things to do, but all of us can be faithful in the little things.

Today's Reading

Go to www.usccb.org/bible/readings for the text or an audio recording of the Scripture readings for the Memorial of Saint Thérèse of the Child Jesus.

Faith-Sharing Activity

Saint Thérèse called herself a "little flower"—not anything great, but still precious to the Lord. In her honor, make a bouquet of tissue paper flowers. Instructions can be easily found through an Internet search. You will need colorful tissue paper, pipe cleaners or flexible wire, scissors, and a vase.

Take your bouquet to a neighbor who might need a bit of cheer, or perhaps to someone in the hospital.

Conversation Starter

How can we show love for God in little ways? Does doing little things for someone else without expecting anything in return mean that we are allowing others to take us for granted? How can we show we appreciate one another and each one's gifts?

Today's Prayer

Lord Jesus, thank you for giving Saint Thérèse such strength in doing little things with great love. Give us those same gifts of strength and love, so that we can appreciate all the little gifts you give to us each day. We ask in your name, Lord Jesus. Amen.

Memorial of Saint Francis of Assisi (October 4)

Introduction

Saint Francis heard God asking him to "Rebuild my church." At first Francis obeyed by restoring the ruined church of the Portiuncula, but later he realized that it would be by the preaching and teaching of his new Franciscan order that the Church would be rebuilt. Pope Francis, in taking the name of this great saint, has made "rebuilding the Church" a priority in our own times, through authentic Gospel living and care for those who are poor.

Today's Reading

Go to www.usccb.org/bible/readings for the text or an audio recording of the Scripture readings for the Memorial of Saint Francis of Assisi.

Faith-Sharing Activity

Plan a family shopping trip solely dedicated to buying supplies for a local food pantry or shelter. Decide ahead of time how much your family would like to spend.

(Each family member might also make a donation to add to the pot.) Also include toiletry items on your list (toothpaste, soap, shampoo, conditioner, etc.). As soon as possible, make a family trip to the food pantry to drop off the items.

Conversation Starter
What is our job in building up the Church? Whom can we care for with love? How can we follow Jesus as Saint Francis did?

Today's Prayer
Saint Francis himself made up this prayer. Let us listen carefully and make it our own. *(Pray the Peace Prayer of Saint Francis on page 101.)*

Memorial of Our Lady of the Rosary (October 7)

Introduction
Today, we celebrate the Memorial of Our Lady of the Rosary. The practice of praying the Rosary grew out of the monastic practice of praying the 150 psalms each week. Those who could not read the psalms were allowed to pray a Hail Mary for each one instead. These prayers were counted on beads, which have evolved into the five-decade chain of rosary beads that we use today. Turn to page 105 to read more about how to pray the Rosary.

Today's Reading
Go to www.usccb.org/bible/readings for the text or an audio recording of the Scripture readings for the Memorial of Our Lady of the Rosary.

Faith-Sharing Activity
There are instructions online for making rosaries from various materials, including knotted twine. Some families enjoy making rosaries for the military or for prisoners. (These must be black or brown.)

For a "refresher course" on praying the rosary, look online for "Rosary coloring pages." There is a nice selection that can be printed. Choose one in which all five decades are pictured. You may want to ask the family to gather around the table and pray a decade of the Rosary while coloring the beads.

Save the coloring pages and "pray and color" another decade each week. Continue every few days until the entire page has been prayed and colored!

Conversation Starter
How can you pray the Rosary without rosary beads?

Some families pray a decade of the Rosary at the beginning of a car trip. Some pray a decade of the Rosary together before going to bed at night. When might your family pray a decade of the Rosary together?

Today's Prayer

In honor of Our Lady, let us pray one more Hail Mary together. Let us ask Mary to be with our family today and every day.

Hail Mary, full of grace, the Lord is with thee.
Blessed art thou among women, and blessed is the fruit of thy womb, Jesus.
Holy Mary, Mother of God,
pray for us sinners, now and at the hour of our death.
Amen.

November

November is a festive month, especially for Americans, who look forward to Thanksgiving near its end. Our Catholic calendar begins November with All Saints' Day and All Souls' Day—two days in which we remember "those who have gone before us with the sign of faith." The primary Marian feast for November is the feast of the Presentation of Our Lady in the Temple. Because Advent usually begins in November, we are also looking ahead to Christmas. (What? Already?)

The special flower designated for November is the chrysanthemum. The "mum" is the flower of cheerfulness and love. In the midst of November's gusty winds and lower temperatures, its cheerfulness is tested and not found wanting! In these autumn days, look for chrysanthemums in pots on front steps and stoops. If possible, put out your own pot!

Solemnity of All Saints
(November 1)

Introduction

Today is the day for all saints, and especially for all those saints who are not commemorated in the Church calendar! Today is the day to thank God for the saintliness of the members of our own families who, after showing us what a good life is, are now living with God. We remember that we are united with them even now, especially when we receive the Body and Blood of Christ in the Eucharist.

Today's Reading

Go to www.usccb.org/bible/readings for the text or an audio recording of the Scripture readings for the Solemnity of All Saints.

Faith-Sharing Activity

Many of us were named after saints. What do you know about your family's baptismal saints? Names of saints can be searched online. Look up the names of family members to find the story behind each name. (Sometimes a saint's name is given as a second name at the time of baptism.)

Find books or movies about some of the saints you have discovered to read and watch together!

Some of us were named after family members as well. Tell the story of the family member after whom you or your children were named.

Conversation Starter

Today's Gospel highlights the Beatitudes, the "blessings" Jesus promises to those who follow him. Think of a family member, relative, or friend (living or dead) who exemplifies a "Beatitude attitude." Take some time to discuss why each person named lives the Beatitudes.

Today's Prayer

God and Father of all the saints, may we learn from those who have gone before us. Help us to share their faith, their hope, and their love. We ask this in the name of Jesus, your Risen Son.
Amen.

The Commemoration of All the Faithful Departed (All Souls' Day, November 2)

Introduction

Today we remember all those who have died, especially in the past year. Parishes often have various ways of commemorating those who have died. Some parishes display lists of remembrance, some display candles, some write out the names of deceased parish members on banners hung in church. The most important way we can remember those who have died is by celebrating the Eucharist, for in Jesus, all are alive. All of us, living or dead, are alive in him.

Today's Reading

Go to www.usccb.org/bible/readings for the text or an audio recording of the Scripture readings for the Commemoration of All the Faithful Departed.

Faith-Sharing Activity

As a family, participate in your parish's remembrance of those who have died.

At home, write a list of deceased loved ones on a piece of paper and display it in a prominent place during the month of November. You may want to gather photos of these loved ones and place them near the list. If possible, visit the family cemetery plot today or on the weekend.

This may be an appropriate time to set up a small family prayer table in a corner of the family room or living room, or even in a bedroom. Include a crucifix (either fixed to a wall or standing) and a statue or icon of Our Lady. The pictures noted above could be displayed here. Gather each night at the altar for a short period of family prayer—perhaps an Our Father, a Hail Mary, and a Glory Be.

Conversation Starter

Do our loved ones still care about us after they die? Can we still talk to them? *(Yes, because they are living in God's infinite and eternal love, they probably care much more about us than they ever did. We can talk to them, pray for them, and even ask their help. They are an important part of the Church, and we are joined with them in the Body of Christ, especially when we receive the Eucharist.)*

Today's Prayer

Father, we pray for those we love who have gone home to you. Make us one in your love. One day, bring us all together into life everlasting.
Amen.

 ## Memorial of the Presentation of the Blessed Virgin Mary (November 21)

Introduction
This feast commemorates the presentation of Mary into the Temple as a three-year-old child. While this feast is based on a legend, it is a foretaste of the truth we celebrate on December 8: that Mary was sinless from the very moment of her conception.

Today's Reading

Go to www.usccb.org/bible/readings for the text or an audio recording of the Scripture readings for the Memorial of the Presentation of the Blessed Virgin Mary.

Faith-Sharing Activity

The "temple" in which we present ourselves each week is our parish church. In that church, at every Eucharist, we renew our dedication to God.

As a family, make a simple drawing of your parish church as follows:

- Take two pieces of 8½-inch x 11-inch paper. Glue them together, on top of each other, by gluing the top and two sides. (Leave the bottom open.) On the top of these two glued-together pieces, draw the front of your church, including the doors. Then cut the doors open by cutting through just the top sheet of paper. Inside the church doors, on the sheet of paper underneath, draw the altar and any statues you might see from the back of the church.

- At the top of the drawing, write the name of your parish church. Underneath, write "The House of God."

- Stand the drawing on your family prayer table.

Conversation Starter

Each woman carrying a baby is carrying a precious child of God. In what ways can we help pregnant women, especially those who are poor? This is a wonderful way to honor Mary!

Today's Prayer

Let us pray to Mary based on the Litany of Loreto, which gives us many special names to call Mary. The response is: Pray for us.

Holy Mother of God, (response)
Mother of the Church, (response)
Ark of the Covenant, (response)
Gate of Heaven, (response)
Help of Christians, (response)
Queen of Families, (response)
Queen of Peace, (response)

 First Sunday of Advent

Introduction

The custom of the Advent wreath in our parishes and homes comes from the German custom of marking each week by lighting candles set within an evergreen wreath. The Christmas tree also comes to us from Germany (by way of Queen Victoria of England's husband, who was German).

Today's Reading

Go to www.usccb.org/bible/readings for the text or an audio recording of the Scripture readings for each Sunday of Advent.

Faith-Sharing Activity

Involve the family in setting up your Advent wreath. While Advent wreath forms can be found for purchase (made of wire or ceramic), you can easily make your own wreath with some evergreen or holly branches and four candlesticks. The candles should be colored ones (three purple and one rose). Some families place a white candle in the middle to symbolize the feast of Christmas. Place the Advent wreath in a prominent place, like the center of the family table. Use the prayer suggested below for the lighting of the Advent wreath each week, preferably on Saturday evening. You may want to light it before supper, and have supper by its light.

Make preparing for Christmas a faith-filled experience. As a family, make a list of your "ideal family Christmas," including family activities, school events, and what your family would like to do for relatives, friends, neighbors, and those in need. Then choose the activities that would mean the most and follow through on them.

Conversation Starter

The Gospel today tells us that the coming of Jesus will be a surprise for us, and that we should keep watch at all times. During Advent we can practice waiting for the surprise of Jesus.

Do you like surprises? Why or why not?

Today's Prayer
An Advent Wreath Prayer

Lord, we gather around this wreath, a circle of unity and love.

As we light this first (*second, third, or last*) candle, help us to remember that you are the Light of the World. Shine on our darkness, and drive out our fears.

As we prepare to celebrate your birth among us, show us the way of hope*. We ask this in your name, Lord Jesus.

Light the candle for this week.
  *Second Sunday's candle: the way of love.
  *Third Sunday's candle (rose): the way of joy.
  *Fourth Sunday's candle: the way of peace.

"Long is our winter, dark is our night.
O come set us free, O saving Light!
Long is our winter, dark is our night.
O come set us free, O saving Light!
Come, set us free, O saving Light!
O come dwell among us,
O saving Light!"

(Advent Round)

December

Some places have had snow already. In other places, snow is coming. In still other places, it is chilly, gray, and cold. December is here. The long, dark nights have begun.

Yet there is hope. At the December equinox (December 21) the days begin to lengthen again. The ancient Romans noticed this and celebrated a Feast of Light around this time. The early Christians thought that this celebration of the light would be a great time to celebrate the coming of the True Light into the world. And so the feast of Christmas was assigned to December 25. Be sure to notice the lengthening days after the feast of Christmas!

But now it is Advent, a time of waiting in darkness. Try to be patient with the waiting times in your life, as Mary and Joseph waited for the birth of Jesus. As your family prepares for Christmas, keep Jesus in your mind and heart, as they did.

The flower for this month is the poinsettia, with its Christmas colors of red and green. Red and green have special meaning. Green is a symbol of eternal life (as evergreens do not shed their leaves but stay green all winter) and red is the sign of Jesus' humanity, for, while truly God, he shares our flesh and blood forever.

 ## Second Sunday of Advent

Introduction

Saint John the Baptist went before Jesus, calling all to prepare for the coming of the Lord. The rough ways that trip us up will be made smooth. We will not have to wait much longer. Our salvation is near, because Jesus is coming soon.

As a family, complete all of the following faith-sharing steps, or do one or more as your time permits.

Today's Reading
Go to www.usccb.org/bible/readings for the text or an audio recording of the Scripture readings for the Second Sunday of Advent.

Faith-Sharing Activity
Bring out the Christmas crèche. With your family, set up all the figures except Mary, Joseph, the donkey, and the Baby Jesus. Place the Baby Jesus figure in a nearby drawer until Christmas Eve. Place Mary, Joseph, and the donkey at the other end of the house. Each day, ask a child to move Mary and Joseph closer to the stable.

Their journey will end on Christmas Eve. In the evening (or after Midnight Mass), place the Baby Jesus figure in the manger.

Conversation Starter
During Advent, we journey with Mary and Joseph as we travel to Bethlehem in a spiritual way. Journeys can be fun but sometimes they are not easy. With your family, recall a few family journeys. How did they bring your family closer together? What did you learn on these journeys?

Today's Prayer
(After you set up your Christmas crèche, pray this prayer of blessing.)

Lord Jesus, bless this Christmas crèche. May it remind us always that you were born as a little child and came to live among us in love and in peace. May we share your peace and love with all we meet.
Amen.

Saint Nicholas Day
(December 6)

Introduction
Saint Nicholas of Myra is the patron of children. As a bishop, he tossed gold coins into the home of a poor family with three daughters, to prevent them from being sold into slavery. The coins landed in stockings drying by the fire. So now we know the origin of Christmas stockings!

Today's Reading
This Gospel may be read for the feast of Saint Nicholas: Mark 10:13–16.

Faith-Sharing Activity
Saint Nicholas is the original Santa Claus! Traditionally, his day is celebrated by having children put their shoes outside their bedroom doors before bed. (Some may want to fill shoes with carrots or hay for Saint Nicholas's donkey.) In the morning, the children find gold-wrapped chocolate coins or other candy inside! A candy cane can represent Saint Nicholas's crozier.

Other ways to celebrate include reading a story about Saint Nicholas; shopping for toys to give to toy drives for poor children; or pledging to give a fixed amount to a favorite children's charity like the Missionary Childhood Association (sponsored by the Vatican). More ideas may be found online by searching "Saint Nicholas Day."

Conversation Starter
Both Saint Nicholas and Santa Claus represent the spirit of giving. Why is giving to others so important? Why is giving to those who have less so important?

Today's Prayer
Saint Nicholas, watch over the children of the world, especially those who are poor, hungry, or in danger. Bring them to Jesus, and help us help those who are in need. Amen.

 ## The Solemnity of the Immaculate Conception (December 8)

Introduction
The term "Immaculate Conception" means that Mary, the Mother of God, was preserved from the stain of original sin from the first moment of her conception. Mary was "saved ahead of time" through the merits of Jesus Christ, who saved the entire human race.

Today's Reading
Go to www.usccb.org/bible/readings for the text or an audio recording of the Scripture readings for the Solemnity of the Immaculate Conception of the Blessed Virgin Mary.

Faith-Sharing Activity
Mary is called "the New Eve" because, unlike the first Eve who disobeyed God, Mary trusted God.

To celebrate Mary's faith, trust, and obedience, make a "New Eve Tree of Life." Find a bare branch from outdoors, or an evergreen branch, and put it in a vase. Cut out several red "apples" from red construction paper. On each paper apple, brainstorm as a family and write a characteristic you admire in Mary. *(Suggestions: faith, trust, hope, etc.)* Tie the apples to the tree with string or twist ties. Place it in the center of your Advent wreath.

Conversation Starter
In the Hail Mary prayer, we pray, "Hail Mary, full of grace." Mary is so full of grace that there is no room for sin. How can we make more room for God's grace and less room for sin? What can help us make more room for God's grace in our lives?

Today's Prayer
"O Mary, conceived without sin, pray for us who have recourse to thee."

(Explain that to "have recourse" means "to turn to for help." You may want to add this prayer to your family's grace before meals this week.)

The Feast of Our Lady of Guadalupe (December 12)

Introduction

In the sixteenth century, in Mexico, the Virgin Mary appeared to a peasant named Juan Diego. She spoke to him in his native Indian dialect, and asked that a shrine be built in her honor. She showed two signs: Juan Diego found roses in December, and on his cloak was left the beautiful picture of Our Lady of Guadalupe. Our Lady's shrine in Mexico City is the now the most visited Catholic pilgrimage site in the world.

Today's Reading

Go to www.usccb.org/bible/readings for the text or an audio recording of the Scripture readings for the Feast of Our Lady of Guadalupe.

Faith-Sharing Activity

Have a Mexican meal today! Find a simple recipe for tacos or other Mexican favorites. Gather the family to help with the preparations. For dessert, you may want to make *flan* or custard, which is known all over South America (and is said to be Pope Francis's very favorite dessert).

It is also traditional to drink hot chocolate on this special feast day.

You may want to participate in a local celebration of Mass, often followed by a festive meal.

Conversation Starter

When Mary appears with a message for us, she always seems to appear to those who are poor and humble. Why do you think this is so? Why do you think she spoke to Juan Diego in his own language? How does this help us to understand how we might spread the Gospel in our own times?

Today's Prayer

Our Lady of Guadalupe, help us to understand others, so that we might bring them to Jesus, as you did.
Amen.

Third Sunday of Advent

Introduction

Rejoice! (Gaudete! in Latin) Today is Gaudete Sunday, its theme of joy taken from the message in today's readings. As of today, we are "halfway to Bethlehem" and the Lord is near! That is cause for rejoicing!

Today's Reading
Go to www.usccb.org/bible/readings for the text or an audio recording of the Scripture readings for the Third Sunday of Advent.

Faith-Sharing Activity
Make a "Family Joy" banner. Find three sheets of plain paper. On the first sheet, print a large open J (to be colored in). On the second sheet, print a large open O. On the third sheet, print a large open Y. Color in the letters with a rose-colored crayon. Around the letter J, have each family member write his or her name. (The names of pets may also be included, as they bring us joy, too!) Around the letter O, write one or two reasons each family member brings joy to all. Around the letter Y, think of challenges to joy for each family member, and write how each can face it. ("I can be more joyful when taking out the garbage because it helps the family—Henry.") Hang or tape the banners in a special place.

Conversation Starter
What would make our family life more joyful this week?

If your parish used rose vestments this weekend, ask the following: Who noticed the color of today's vestments? Why did the color of the vestments change from Advent purple? *(The rose-colored vestments reflect the theme of "rejoicing.")*

Today's Prayer
Jesus, you are our joy, and you are near. Without anxiety, we make our requests to you. Guard our hearts and minds in your peace.
Amen.

Las Posadas
(December 16–December 24)

Introduction

"Las Posadas" is a nine-day celebration before Christmas. The word posada *means "lodging" in Spanish. For nine evenings, two people (Mary and Joseph) lead a procession as they seek to find shelter. They go to a particular house and hear "No, we have no room." When "the innkeeper" finally lets them in, every-one comes inside for a festive evening, beginning with prayer.*

Today's Reading

The custom of *Las posadas* is based on the Christmas story in the Gospel of Luke (Luke 2:1–7).

Faith-Sharing Activity

The nine evenings of Las Posadas are a novena (a nine-day period of prayer). They also represent the nine months of Mary's pregnancy. In these days before Christmas, we think of all the women in the world about to give birth. What can we do to help women who may not have all that they need to welcome their babies? Find a group or charity that will accept new or used infant clothing and accessories. Imagine the joy of a new mother as she wraps her baby in a soft and cozy blanket!

Conversation Starter

A special song is sung during *las posadas*. It is a dialogue song. The "innkeeper" sings:

"Is that you, Joseph? Is that you, Mary? Enter pilgrims. I didn't recognize you."

Do we recognize those who are in need? Why or why not? How can we "let them in" to our lives?

Today's Prayer

Jesus, Mary, and Joseph,

We welcome you not only into our homes but also into our hearts. May we recognize you in the faces of those who are poor and in need.
Amen.

Fourth Sunday of Advent

Introduction

Some of us say, "At last!" Others say, "Already?" In some years, the Fourth Sunday of Advent begins a very short week, as Christmas Eve is around the corner! As the old saying goes, "Prepare your hearts!"

Today's Reading

Go to www.usccb.org/bible/readings for the text or an audio recording of the Scripture readings for the Fourth Sunday of Advent.

Faith-Sharing Activity

Today's Gospel recalls the visit of Mary to Elizabeth. Mary intended to help Elizabeth, yet it was Mary who was blessed and comforted by Elizabeth! This often happens when we visit someone in need—we receive unexpected blessings in return. Make plans as a family to visit someone in need this week, either before or after Christmas. It may be a neighbor, an elderly person in a retirement center, or someone your parish priest or administrator might suggest. Bring a Christmas card with you, signed by all family members. Make a Christmas connection with someone who may need company this week. Step out in faith, as Mary did, and receive a blessing!

Conversation Starter

Visitors are a blessing. Saint Benedict wrote in his Rule, "Let every guest be received like Christ." How do we show visitors that they are a blessing to us? How can we be a blessing to others when we visit them?

Today's Prayer

(Explain that the Hail Mary prayer comes from Elizabeth's words to Mary in today's Gospel.

Pray a Hail Mary together, asking Our Lady to help you prepare for the coming of Jesus into your hearts at Christmas.)

Christmas Eve
(December 24)

Introduction

Christmas Eve! Family traditions on this day differ. Some families have a special time of opening presents tonight, by the light of the Christmas tree. Other families wait until Christmas Day for their festivities. Whatever your Christmas tradition, it will be a source of blessing and joy for your family!

Today's Reading

Go to www.usccb.org/bible/readings for the text or an audio recording of the Scripture readings for December 25, the Nativity of the Lord. There you will find the readings for the Vigil Mass (the early evening Mass on December 24).

Faith-Sharing Activity

Some families keep the custom of setting up the Christmas tree on Christmas Eve. The Christmas tree is a sign of faith, a sign that the Light of the World has come to dwell among us. Be sure to place the figure of the Infant Jesus in the crèche tonight!

You may want to dim the lights and sing "Silent Night" around the crèche before the family goes to sleep tonight. The holy infant has come to bring joy to the world!

Conversation Starter

There are just a few more hours before Christmas Day. What have we learned during this time of preparation? What is most important for our family to celebrate on this happy day?

Today's Prayer

Blessing of a Christmas Tree

Lord Jesus, bless this festive tree that brings us joy as we celebrate your birth. As a sign of everlasting life, may it remind us that you are always and ever the Light of the World.
Amen.

 Christmas Day
(December 25)

Introduction

Christmas Day is the only day of the year in which three Masses are celebrated, with three different sets of readings. The Gospel at the Midnight Mass tells the story of the birth of Jesus. The Mass at Dawn is sometimes called "The Shepherds' Mass" because their story is told in that Gospel. The Gospel of the Mass During the Day emphasizes that the Word of God has come to dwell among us.

Today's Reading

Go to www.usccb.org/bible/readings for the text or an audio recording of the Scripture readings for December 25, the Nativity of the Lord. There you will find the readings for the Mass During the Night (Midnight Mass), Mass at Dawn (the Early-Morning Mass), and Mass During the Day.

Faith-Sharing Activity

Before this festive day ends, you may want to read one of today's Gospels aloud, or share the Christmas story through attractive books written for children. This reflective pause may become a Christmas tradition!

As a family, write a "Christmas card" to Jesus. Thank him for coming to live among us as our Savior. Have all sign the card, then place it near the crèche.

Conversation Starter

What difference would it have made to the world if Jesus had not come to tell us and show us God's love? What difference does Jesus make in our lives today? How can we share his love with others?

Today's Prayer

Merry Christmas, Jesus! And Happy Birthday! Thank you for coming to us as a little child, and living among us to show us God's love.
Amen.

The Feast of the Holy Family of Jesus, Mary, and Joseph (The Sunday after Christmas)

Introduction

Today the liturgy fast-forwards us to a Gospel scene of Jesus at age twelve. Even today, at age twelve or thirteen, a Jewish boy is expected to take increasing responsibility for his life. Yet, in the Holy Family, it seems there was a breakdown in communication, which caused "great anxiety" (see Luke 2:41–52). Yes, it happens in the best of families!

Today's Reading

Go to www.usccb.org/bible/readings for the text or an audio recording of the Scripture readings for the Feast of the Holy Family.

Faith-Sharing Activity

Prepare sheets of paper with one family member's name written at the top of each sheet. Call the family together around the table. Ask each family member to write ways the person named contributes to family life, whether in physical ways *(e.g., preparing meals)* or in more intangible ways *(keeping calm in stressful situations)*. Send the papers around the table at least three times.

Read the sheets aloud. At the bottom of each sheet, write, "Thank you, [name]!" Post the sheets in a special place where they will be seen often this week.

Conversation Starter

How do you think Mary and Joseph felt when Jesus was lost and they did not know where he was? How do you think Jesus felt when his mother and Joseph found him? Why is good communication necessary in our family?

Today's Prayer
A Family Blessing

Father in Heaven, you created us to love and care for one another in families. Bless our family, and help us to love and support one another always.
Amen.

January

January is two-faced. Like its namesake, the god Janus, one of its faces looks back at the old year and the other looks forward to the new. So it is not surprising that we might feel a little bit torn in January, maybe even a little regretful that the past year is gone, with its unique gifts and opportunities. Or, we may look back with relief and say, "Thank you, God, for helping me through a rough year. I'm glad it's behind me!" But sometimes, it is only in looking back that we see that God was truly with us, all along.

In January, we look forward to a new year like an unopened gift. We will open it, day by day, even moment by moment. What will the New Year bring? We cannot know, even as we cannot really predict what will happen today or tomorrow.

But, as we continue to celebrate the Christmas season, the coming of the Word made flesh, we do know this: God is with us. In our joys, our sorrows, in family life, in the care and concern of friends, God is with us. He is with us especially when we celebrate the Eucharist, and receive within us the great gift of his Son, in the Body and Blood of Christ.

The flower for January is the carnation. It takes its name from the Greek word for "coronation," which is related to "flower garlands." Jesus came among us to make us not only his servants, but also his friends; to make us not only his friends, but his brothers and sisters. Through Baptism, we are children of the Father. Maybe we should start the year by wearing crowns of carnations!

 ## New Year's Eve
(December 31)

Introduction
New Year's Eve is not a liturgical feast. The readings today are for the seventh day after Christmas. But sometimes it is good to be reminded that the real "identity" of a day, according to the Church calendar, is beyond time and expresses eternal truth. Yet, today we can reflect on the year that is past, and express our prayerful hopes for the year to come.

Today's Reading
Go to www.usccb.org/bible/readings for the text or an audio recording of the Scripture readings for the Seventh Day in the Octave of Christmas.

Faith-Sharing Activity

The gift of a new year is something to be celebrated. Promise younger children that you will wake them up at ten minutes to midnight so that they can see the new year in. Set noisemakers (or wooden spoons, pots, and pans) near the door so that they may step outside and welcome the new year with joyful noise. If your town's church bells are rung at midnight, remind everyone to listen for the bells.

Or, set an earlier time for your celebration (just before regular bedtime). It's midnight somewhere!

Conversation Starter

As we say goodbye to the year that is past, and welcome the new year, what good things in the past year can we thank God for?

Today's Prayer

God our Father, thank you for the gift of the past year, with all its joys and sorrows. As we look forward to the year that is to come, give us your peace, knowing that all of our days are in your hands. We ask in the name of Jesus. Amen.

 New Year's Day (January 1, The Octave Day of Christmas, Solemnity of the Blessed Virgin Mary, the Mother of God)

Introduction

Only Christmas and Easter have an octave (an eight-day celebration) after the feast, and this is the last day of the octave of Christmas. Today's feast has been celebrated in honor of Mary, the Mother of God (Theotokos in Greek) since the seventh century. Displaced by the feast of the Circumcision of Jesus in the thirteenth century, this feast was restored in 1974.

Today's Reading

Go to www.usccb.org/bible/readings for the text or an audio recording of the Scripture readings for the Octave Day of Christmas, the Solemnity of the Blessed Virgin Mary.

Faith-Sharing Activity

The Church also observes this day as a "World Day of Peace." Write the names of various countries on small pieces of paper, especially those countries in which there is tension or war. Ask each family member to draw the name of one country to "adopt" in prayer during the coming year. Help one another decide on a prayer commitment. For example, each family member might promise to say three Hail Marys a day for peace in the country drawn. You may want to decide where and when to pray these prayers together.

Conversation Starter

What can we do to make our family life more peaceful? What can we do to help people live in peace in our town and in our country? What can we do to encourage peace in the world?

Today's Prayer

God, enlighten our hearts and minds to choose your paths. Show us the way of peace. In the name of your Son, the Prince of Peace.
Amen.

The Epiphany of the Lord (Sunday after the Octave of Christmas)

Introduction

Today's feast predates the feast of Christmas, and, in some countries in the world, this is the day for exchanging gifts. The original date of this feast is January 6, and the Magi (the Three Kings or Wise Men) are still honored on that date in popular celebrations.

Today's Reading

Go to www.usccb.org/bible/readings for the text or an audio recording of the Scripture readings for the Epiphany of the Lord.

Faith-Sharing Activity

The blessing of homes has been traditionally reserved for the feast of the Epiphany. In some parishes, blessed chalk is distributed so that families can mark their door-ways with the initials of the Three Kings. (If you do not have blessed chalk, ordinary chalk can be used.) Gather your family at the front door.

Begin: The three Wise Men, **C**aspar, **M**elchior, and **B**althazar, followed a star to find the Christ Child. May Christ bless us, our home, and our journeys this year.

Write on the top of the door (or near the door): 20 + C + M + B + __ __ [last two digits of the year].

Pray: O Lord, bless this house, all who live here, all who visit here, and all who will pass through our doors in the coming year. May we share your love and peace with all. Amen.

Conversation Starter

God's beautiful world gives us clues about him. What clues about God do you see in his creation?

Today's Prayer

Lord Jesus, help us to follow you by following the inspirations, the good thoughts, the Holy Spirit sends to us. We ask in your name.
Amen.

The Baptism of the Lord (The Last Day of the Christmas Season)

Introduction

Today's celebration marks the end of the Christmas Season and the beginning of Ordinary Time. Today, we celebrate the baptism of Jesus and the manifestation of the mystery of the Holy Trinity: the Father, the Son, and the Holy Spirit. God is at work among us!

Today's Reading

Go to www.usccb.org/bible/readings for the text or an audio recording of the Scripture readings for the Baptism of the Lord.

Faith-Sharing Activity

Today Jesus is affirmed as the beloved Son of the Father, and is supported by the Holy Spirit. Life goes better when we also affirm and support one another. Take time to do this by giving each family member a piece of paper. Ask them to write their names lengthwise on the paper, one letter under another. Together think of positive or affirming words or phrases for each letter of each person's name. For example: DAN: D=diligent; A=amusing; N=neatness devotee. (Use the entire name to make a longer affirmation.) Post the papers in a special place for all to see this week.

Conversation Starter

We are all God's beloved children. How does that make you feel? How do God's beloved children act toward all of the other children of God in the world?

Today's Prayer

Thank you, Lord, for giving us this beautiful Christmas Season to celebrate your birth and your living among us. Help us to follow you in your mission of love and care for others.
Amen.

February

"Don't make any big decisions in February!" This saying reminds us that February is apt to be a gloomy month, clouding our vision and bending our mood toward pessimism. Winter hangs on, and we might tend to think, of any endeavor in which we are involved, "Oh, what's the use? I may as well give up."

This would be a mistake. While February tends to pull the wool over our eyes, hiding the goodness of our lives from us, it also carries within it the promise of spring. This is the message of February's flower, the violet. Low to the ground, humble, yet remarkably resilient (always returning after a long winter), violets symbolize what must be our attitude in February: humble, faithful, ready to just "show up." The name *violet* may come from the Latin word *vias*, meaning "wayside." The violet accompanies our journey from winter to spring, bearing hope in its unobtrusive loveliness.

February's feast days carry hope as well. The Feast of the Presentation of the Lord in the Temple (Candlemas) reminds us that the Light is still with us. Valentine's Day, although no longer an official liturgical feast, reminds us of God's gifts of human love and friendship. Finally, we celebrate Ash Wednesday with ashes on our foreheads and a dawning realization in our hearts: God is giving us another chance. We can begin again. And, if Lent is here, then spring really is coming. After all, the word *Lent* comes from an Anglo-Saxon word meaning "lengthen." And lengthening days mean spring!

 ## Feast of the Presentation of the Lord (February 2)

Introduction
Today's feast is also called Candlemas because it celebrates the coming of Jesus, "A light for revelation for the Gentiles" (Luke 2:32). The Church celebrates with a candle procession.

Today's Reading
Go to www.usccb.org/bible/readings for the text or an audio recording of the Scripture readings for the Feast of the Presentation of the Lord.

Faith-Sharing Activity
To celebrate the Light of the World with candles, have your evening meal by candle-

light. Candles make any meal a special occasion!

Or, with your family, make your own cardboard candles to celebrate this day. You will need a cardboard egg carton, empty toilet paper rolls, and construction paper in white and yellow. Make a base for each candle by cutting apart the egg carton so that each candle has a base with a spoke to brace it. Wrap each toilet paper roll in white paper. Cut out a yellow flame, with a tab at the bottom. Tape the tabs inside the rolls so that the flames stick up. Set each paper candle over a spoke. You may want to write the name of Jesus on each candle. Place a paper candle at each family member's place.

Conversation Starter
The Light of Christ is reflected in the lengthening days. Jesus told us that we, too, are the light of the world. How can we bring light to our family, our parish, our town or city?

Today's Prayer
Lord, at the end of every day, your Church prays: Let us go in peace, for today we have seen your salvation. Thank you, Lord, our Light, for saving us today.
Amen.

Ash Wednesday (The Beginning of the Lenten Observance)

Introduction
The Lenten observance begins today, with the Church's reminder that life is short, and the time for Gospel living is now. To repent means to change, and our Lenten fasting is a small change we make to help us make bigger, lasting changes in our lives. (See the Lenten regulations after Today's Prayer.)

Today's Reading
Go to www.usccb.org/bible/readings for the text or an audio recording of the Scripture readings for Ash Wednesday.

Faith-Sharing Activity
Make a simple Lenten calendar. Cut out a large cross from light cardboard (like a cereal box). Trace on purple construction paper, cut out, and glue to one side. Trace on yellow construction paper, cut out, and glue to the other side. On the purple side,

write the following numbers: At the top of the cross, 1; at the left arm, 2; at the right, 3; at the bottom, 4; in the middle, 5. On the yellow side, write "Holy" at the top and "Week" at the bottom. Across the two arms, write *CHRIST IS RISEN!* Place this calendar where it will be seen each day. As the Lenten weeks go by, cross off the numbers and "Holy Week." On Easter Sunday, the message will shine: Christ is risen!

Conversation Starter

As a family, consider not only what you will give up for Lent (for example, saving money for a donation to those who are poor) but what you will do for others for Lent.

Today's Prayer

Lord Jesus, help us to walk in your footsteps this Lent. Help us say no to selfishness and yes to the needs of others.
Amen.

The Lenten Regulations

1. *For those Catholics aged 18 to 59, fasting is required on Ash Wednesday and Good Friday.*

Fasting means that no food is taken between meals, and that one full meal is allowed. Two smaller meals may be taken, but they may not equal one full meal.

If possible, the fast on Good Friday is continued until the Easter Vigil (on Holy Saturday night) as the "paschal fast" to honor the suffering and death of the Lord Jesus, and to prepare ourselves to share more fully in and to celebrate more readily his Resurrection.

Those who would jeopardize their health by fasting (pregnant or nursing women, those with chronic diseases like diabetes) should not fast.

2. *For those Catholics aged 14 and over, abstinence from meat is required on Ash Wednesday and Good Friday, and on all the Fridays of Lent.*

Comment: Needless to say, indulging in lavish seafood buffets on the Fridays of Lent misses the penitential point of abstinence. Our fasting and abstinence remind us of the sacrifice of Jesus' life, and are ways to unite our sacrifice to his in thought and prayer.

SPRING

Now the green blade rises from the buried grain,
Wheat that in dark earth many days has lain;
Love lives again, that with the dead has been;
Love is come again, like wheat that springeth green.

When our hearts are wintry, grieving, or in pain,
Your touch can call us back to life again;
Fields of our hearts that dead and bare have been:
Love is come again, like wheat that springeth green.

(J.M.C. Crum, 1872–1958)

 **March**

If it comes in like a lion, it will go out like a lamb. Or, if it comes in like a lamb, it will go out like a lion. This is the folk wisdom that defines March. How true is it this year?

The lion and lamb metaphors are apt for spring, which begins on March 19, 20, or 21 every year. These are the possible dates for the spring equinox, the day when the hours of daylight and darkness are roughly equal. From this point on, the days get longer, the weather gets warmer, and spring bursts upon the world! For, as we recall, "lent" means "lengthening," as in the lengthening days of spring.

Yes, the Season of Lent continues. For the sake of convenience, we have included all the Sundays of Lent in this month of March (although Lent often begins in February and lasts until mid-April). The special feasts of March—Saint Patrick's Day, Saint Joseph's Day, and the Feast of the Annunciation—follow these Lenten Sundays. Then, in April, we consider Holy Week, Good Friday, Easter Sunday, and the Sundays of the Easter Season.

March's flower, the daffodil or jonquil, is an apt Easter flower. Its yellow or white trumpet seems to dispense silent alleluias to the world. The extremes of spring do not defeat it, as it bends gracefully under snow and then bounces back to reflect the springtime sun. It is truly a flower of resurrection.

Just as surely as spring resurrects the earth, so does the season of Lent lead us to the Resurrection of Christ. How wonderfully our world reflects God's action in our lives!

 First Sunday of Lent

Introduction

Today, we follow Jesus into the desert. But we do not go alone. The entire Church is with us for this forty-day desert experience, this forty-day retreat, this forty-day time of prayer, fasting, and almsgiving.

As a family, complete all of the following faith-sharing steps, or do one or more as your time permits.

Today's Reading

Go to www.usccb.org/bible/readings for the text or an audio recording of the Scripture readings for the First Sunday of Lent.

Faith-Sharing Activity

If your parish participates in Operation Rice Bowl (sponsored by Catholic Relief Services), consider joining in. Or make your own special donations box from an empty tissue box, coffee tin, or similar container. Label it *Our Family Gift*. If your family has decided to give up pizza, ice cream, or other treats, calculate how much you are saving by not indulging during Lent. Put that amount of money in your box each week, and, at the end of Lent, count up your savings. Then donate the money to your parish soup kitchen or other charity.

Conversation Starter

How can our family spend a few extra minutes in prayer each day?

How can we fast as a family—not only from food, but also perhaps from TV, phone use, or other distractions?

What will we do instead?

Today's Prayer

Lord Jesus, as we follow you into the desert, help us to open our hearts to your message of love. Help us to help others as we pray, fast, and give alms this Lent. Amen.

 ## Second Sunday of Lent

Introduction

Today, Jesus reveals his glory to his disciples. Perhaps he wanted to encourage them as the days of his passion and death drew near. Again, God the Father assures his Son that, hard as his path will be, he is the beloved.

Today's Reading

Go to www.usccb.org/bible/readings for the text or an audio recording of the Scripture readings for the Second Sunday of Lent.

Faith-Sharing Activity

Who among your immediate or extended family or friends is going through a hard time? Perhaps someone has lost a job. Perhaps someone is in the hospital, or is dealing with a difficult family situation. Perhaps someone has lost a loved one in death. As a family, choose an appropriate card and write a note of encouragement. Assure your family member or friend of your love. In the coming week, invite that person to your home to share a meal.

Conversation Starter

Today's Gospel tells us to listen to Jesus. How do we listen to Jesus? When do we listen to Jesus? Take a moment to listen to Jesus. What is he saying to you?

Today's Prayer

Lord Jesus, we would like to stay with you on the mountain and share your glory. But you send us back to our own homes and neighborhoods to listen to you and to share your message. Help us follow you on the path you set before us.
Amen.

 ## Third Sunday of Lent

Introduction

Today, Jesus compares his own body to the Temple in Jerusalem, the holy place of worship. No matter how holy the Temple is, it is finite. It can be destroyed. But his Body can never be destroyed. The Temple of his Body will be raised up and will live forever. And so will ours.

Today's Reading

Go to www.usccb.org/bible/readings for the text or an audio recording of the Scripture readings for the Third Sunday of Lent. These reflections are based on the usual Lenten readings (not the readings selected for the RCIA Scrutinies).

Faith-Sharing Activity

The number three is a symbolic number. Jesus will spend three days in the tomb before his Resurrection. As Catholics, we have three special prayers that we pray often.

From a piece of light cardboard, cut out three circles for each family member. On one circle, write "Our Father." On the next circle, write "Hail Mary." On the last circle write, "Glory Be." Put the circles in a special place. Invite each person to pray each prayer once each day and then turn the circle over. At the end of the day, all the circles should be blank side out. Turn them over again to prepare for the next day's prayer.

Conversation Starter

Our parish church is God's house. How do we act in God's house? What special actions do we do to show that we know it is a special place?

Today's Prayer

Lord Jesus, you teach us that your house is a house of prayer. Teach us to pray with listening hearts, in sincerity and truth. Amen.

Fourth Sunday of Lent

Introduction
In today's Gospel, Nicodemus comes by night to hear Jesus' teaching about living in the truth and living in the light! Those who do wrong hate the light and love the darkness. Jesus calls his followers to follow him in the light of truth.

Today's Reading
Go to www.usccb.org/bible/readings for the text or an audio recording of the Scripture readings for the Fourth Sunday of Lent (not the readings selected for the RCIA Scrutinies).

Faith-Sharing Activity
As a sign of following Jesus into the light, make paper lanterns. Use yellow or orange construction paper. Fold one sheet in half at its width. Starting from the fold, use scissors to make a line of cuts through the folded sheets, almost down to the edge of the paper. Open the paper and tape the two ends together at top and bottom to make a round lantern. Take one length (about ½ inch wide) of construction paper and tape a handle at the top. One lantern can make a centerpiece, or you may want to hang several lanterns from string across a doorway. Tape the handles to the string so that the lanterns will not slide.

Conversation Starter
Sometimes, when we do something wrong, we feel like hiding. Jesus says, "Come into the light." We can ask forgiveness. What else can we do to come into the light after we have done something wrong?

Today's Prayer
Jesus, you have called us out of darkness into your wonderful light. Help us live in the light and walk in the truth. Help us follow you from darkness into light.
Amen.

Fifth Sunday of Lent

Introduction
Jesus and his teaching are becoming known beyond the boundaries of his home country. "The Greeks" came from a foreign land. They are proof that Jesus will indeed draw all people to himself.

Today's Reading
Go to www.usccb.org/bible/readings for the text or an audio recording of the Scripture readings for the Fifth Sunday of Lent (not the readings selected for the RCIA Scrutinies).

Faith-Sharing Activity
In this Gospel, Jesus tells us that a seed must die in order to bear fruit. A plant starts from a seed. To help the plant grow, the seed disappears, or "dies." Illustrate this dying and rising by watching a bean seed germinate. Take a plastic zip lock baggie. Dampen a paper towel and put it in the baggie. The towel should be damp but not dripping wet. Place a dry bean seed on top of the towel and seal the bag. (No air is needed in the bag.) Tape each bag to a sunny window or wall. The seed needs more warmth than light, so make sure the spot is warm. The seed should germinate in 3 to 5 days. Notice what is happening to the seed. If the towel dries out, moisten it again. After about two weeks, the seed should have sprouted leaves. Plant it in a pot with potting soil.

Conversation Starter
Being unselfish toward others is not always easy. Can you think of times when being unselfish is hard? How is this being like Jesus?

Today's Prayer
Lord Jesus, you are our Seed and our Nourishment. You died to give us life. Help us bear good fruit and share that good fruit with others.
Amen.

The Feast of Saint Patrick (March 17)

Introduction
Happy Saint Patrick's Day! The readings given in the Irish Lectionary for today's celebration are: Sirach 39:6–10; 2 Timothy 4:1–8; and Matthew 13:24–32.

Today's Reading
Go to www.usccb.org/bible/readings for the text or an audio recording of the Scripture readings for today's date. The readings will be Lenten readings.

Faith-Sharing Activity
This is a famous Irish blessing: "May the road rise to meet you. May the wind be ever at your back. And may the Lord hold you in the hollow of his hand."

Make a "blessing chain." Cut many strips of green, white, and orange construction paper, about 8 inches long and 1 inch wide. (Green, white, and orange are the colors of the Irish flag.) On a green strip, write the first sentence of the blessing above. Make a circle with the strip and staple it together. On a white strip, write the second sentence. Circle the strip into the first circle, and staple it together. On an orange strip, write the third sentence. Circle that strip into the second circle. Continue to make a long chain. Hang it across a doorway or loop it from a light fixture.

Conversation Starter
The Irish people "kept the faith" and spread it all over the world. Can we hold onto our faith and share it with others, whether convenient or not? Give some examples.

Today's Prayer
Strengthen us, O Lord, by the Sacrament of the Eucharist, so that we may profess the faith taught by Saint Patrick and proclaim it in our lives. Through Christ our Lord. Amen.

The Solemnity of Saint Joseph (March 19)

Introduction
Saint Joseph is the husband of the Blessed Virgin Mary and the foster-father of Jesus. But it was not until 1962 that Saint John XXIII had Joseph's name inserted into the First Eucharistic Prayer at Mass. Pope Benedict XVI and Pope Francis declared that Joseph's name should be mentioned in all four Eucharistic Prayers.

Today's Reading
Go to www.usccb.org/bible/readings for the text or an audio recording of the Scripture readings for the Solemnity of Saint Joseph.

Faith-Sharing Activity
With your family, make a Saint Joseph mobile as a reminder of the virtues and characteristics of Saint Joseph. Cut the following symbols from construction paper and tie them, by varying lengths of string, to a hanger.

- A white cloud: Joseph listened to God and heard God's message through dreams.
- A yellow angel: An angel spoke to Joseph in a dream.
- A grey donkey: Joseph and Mary journeyed to Bethlehem and to Egypt on a donkey.
- A brown cave or stable: Joseph and Mary found refuge, and Jesus was born.
- A black saw: Joseph was a carpenter and worked with wood.
- A yellow scroll symbolizing God's Law: Joseph was a sincere follower of God's law.

Conversation Starter

When Joseph didn't understand something, he prayed, and God made things clear to him. Are there things in your life that you don't understand? When can you talk to God about them?

Today's Prayer

Thank you, God, for Saint Joseph. Help us to follow his example of listening to you and of moving forward in obedience. We ask in the name of Jesus.
Amen.

 ## The Solemnity of the Annunciation of the Lord (March 25)

Introduction

At the Annunciation, the Angel Gabriel appeared to Mary and asked her to be the Mother of the Son of God, Jesus. On this day, God became human in the womb of a young virgin. We celebrate the Birth of Jesus exactly nine months from today, on December 25.

Today's Reading

Go to www.usccb.org/bible/readings for the text or an audio recording of the Scripture readings for the Solemnity of the Annunciation.

Faith-Sharing Activity

It is traditional in some cultures to bake a special Annunciation cake. Before baking, wrap a coin (like a quarter) in wax paper and place in the dough. Before serving the cake, place a Christmas-crib figure of Mary and an angel, with four white candles, on top. Make a paper crown, cut from bright green construction paper and stapled at the back. Cut tulip shapes from red and pink paper; cut stems and leaves from light green paper. Paste or staple the tulip shapes around the crown, alternating the pink and red flowers. Light the candles, then blow them out and cut the cake. The person who receives the coin receives the flower crown to wear. The coin is a symbol of our salvation, because Christ bought us back and opened Heaven to us. The crown symbolizes the joy of Heaven. The feast of the Annunciation is the beginning of our salvation.

Conversation Starter

The angel shared good news with Mary. Do you have good news to share today? What is it? Why is it important to share good news with others?

Today's Prayer

(Pray the Angelus prayer at 6 a.m., noon, or 6 p.m. today. See pages 99-100 for the Angelus.)

April

April showers bring May flowers! April can be a showery month, and even a snowy month in some parts of the country. Yet it is a flowery month as well, as spring bulbs and bushes burst into bloom.

April carries with it, much of the time, both the Passion and the victory of Christ. In one short week, we travel with Jesus into the darkest hours of his human experience, and then into his most powerful and triumphant one. The Easter Vigil begins an entire six-week season of rejoicing. And it all begins, usually, in April.

Perhaps April's flower, the daisy, is an apt symbol for both perseverance in adversity and Resurrection victory. This sturdy flower seems to grow almost anywhere, and even has a secret message for us if we pluck its petals: "He (or she) loves me . . . He (or she) loves me not." We can be sure that, in the death and Resurrection of Jesus, the message God sends us is always, "He loves me."

Palm Sunday of the Lord's Passion (The Beginning of Holy Week)

Introduction
Today, Sunday, begins in triumph and palms of victory and ends, on Thursday and Friday, in agony and betrayal. Today's Gospel of the Passion gives us an overview of what we can expect. How quickly "Hosanna!" becomes "Crucify him!"

Today's Reading
Go to www.usccb.org/bible/readings for the text or an audio recording of the Scripture readings for Palm Sunday of the Lord's Passion.

Faith-Sharing Activity
Distribute your blessed palms in significant places around your house, as a sign of God's blessing. Tuck one behind a crucifix. Place one on the prayer table. You might even lay one on the dashboard of your car. Palms are a sign of the honor we owe to God, and his blessing. In some of the Eastern Churches (particularly in Europe and Russia), local flowering plants are used instead of palms. Pussy willows are a particular favorite. In other countries, palms are placed in every field or barn, to ask God's blessing on the planting and the harvest.

With your family, if weather permits, take a walk today in a nearby park or nature preserve. Notice the spring flowers. Be grateful for the renewal of the earth. As a family, ask God to renew your faith, hope, and love as Easter approaches.

Reserve time this week for coloring Easter eggs!

Conversation Starter
If Jesus came to our town today, how would we welcome him? Would we have a parade?

Jesus comes to us in every Mass, in Holy Communion. How do we welcome him?

Today's Prayer
Hosanna to the Son of David! Blessed is he who comes in the name of the Lord! Especially in Holy Communion! And in those who are in need!
Amen.

 Holy Thursday

Introduction
Holy Thursday's Mass of the Lord's Supper is a joyous celebration, for on this night Jesus gave us himself in the Eucharist and gave us the priesthood, with its sacramental power. The bells are rung during the Gloria, and then are silent until the Easter celebration. As the Mass ends, we follow Jesus into the Garden of Gethsemane and keep vigil with him.

Today's Reading
Go to www.usccb.org/bible/readings for the text or an audio recording of the Scripture readings for the Evening Mass of the Lord's Supper.

Faith-Sharing Activity
A traditional Holy Thursday custom is to visit several churches (some say three, others seven, or even nine). This may be inspired by the silent vigil that begins in parish churches on Holy Thursday night and often lasts until Friday morning.

Another custom in which the entire family can participate is the cleaning of the house on the first three days of Holy Week, in preparation for the final solemn days of Holy Thursday, Good Friday, and Easter. This recalls the Jewish custom of cleaning the house before celebrating Passover. It seems to be a universal instinct before a big celebration!

Conversation Starter
Today Jesus gave "First Communion" to his Apostles. What did Jesus say to them? How do you think they felt? When you go to Mass, you are at the Last Supper!

Today's Prayer
Thank you, Jesus, for giving us yourself in the Eucharist. May we always appreciate the gift of your Body and Blood, under the appearances of bread and wine. Amen.

Good Friday of the Lord's Passion

Introduction
Today is the only day of the year when the Holy Sacrifice of the Mass is not celebrated. The liturgy today is a meditation on the Passion of Our Lord and a Communion service. We unite with Christ in his sacrifice on the Cross.

Today's Reading
Go to www.usccb.org/bible/readings for the text or an audio recording of the Scripture readings for Good Friday.

Faith-Sharing Activity
Good Friday is a day of fast and abstinence, but your breakfast might include hot cross buns. This is the traditional day for eating them.

In addition to the Solemn Celebration of the Lord's Passion, it is the custom in some places to participate in the Stations of the Cross or the Living Stations of the Cross. You might like to look for one of these celebrations near you.

Today is a day of prayerful silence, especially between the hours of 12 noon and 3 p.m., when the liturgy is usually celebrated. Television, music, unnecessary phone use, and loud play should be eliminated. Use this quiet time to make stained glass paper symbols. With basic glue, paste small squares of tissue paper to a piece of waxed paper. Seal with a layer of glue. When dry, cut the paper into crosses, doves, eggs, or other shapes, and hang them in your windows. Other ideas can be found online by searching "Good Friday children's activities."

Conversation Starter
Today Jesus died for us. What do you want to say to Jesus today? What will happen next, and when do we celebrate it?

Today's Prayer
Lord Jesus, today we remember your Death. Thank you for giving your life for us. We know you did it because you love us. We love you, too.
Amen.

 Easter Sunday

> ### Introduction
> *Christ has died. Alleluia! Christ is risen. Alleluia! Christ will come again. Alleluia! Alleluia! Alleluia!*

Today's Reading
Go to www.usccb.org/bible/readings for the text or an audio recording of the Scripture readings for the Resurrection of the Lord, the Mass of Easter Day.

Faith-Sharing Activity
In order to impress children with the importance of this day, some families make "Resurrection gardens" with a cave, artificial flowers, and Easter figures (the soldiers, the angels, Mary Magdalene, and the Resurrected Jesus). The Easter event can then be told again and again with appropriate action figures!

Have a traditional "battle of the eggs." Two people each take an Easter egg. Whose egg is the strongest? One taps the other's egg on the tip. Then it is the other's turn to tap. The person with the winning egg (no breaks or only one) may be allowed to take the other's egg. The winning egg may go on to challenge others. It is probably best if all eggs are donated to the making of egg salad!

Children enjoy an Easter egg hunt, either in the house or outdoors. Ask older children to hide the eggs.

Conversation Starter
What amazing thing happened today? What was so amazing about it? What does it mean for us one day?

Today's Prayer
Lord Jesus, we never could have imagined your Resurrection! It shows us that you have conquered death, that death is not the final word. You are the final Word, living and true!
Amen. Alleluia!

The Sundays of the Easter Season

Introduction

There are seven weeks in the Easter season, and so there are seven Sundays. On the seventh Sunday, the Ascension of the Lord may be celebrated (although some dioceses keep this feast on the traditional date of the Thursday of the Sixth Week of Easter).

Today's Reading

Go to www.usccb.org/bible/readings for the text or an audio recording of the Scripture readings for each Sunday of the Easter Season.

Faith-Sharing Activity

Each Sunday of the Easter Season reflects an aspect of the Risen Christ, present with us. Plan now to make each of the seven Sundays a "little Easter" in some way. On one Sunday, take a picnic to a favorite park or nature preserve; on another Sunday, declare "ice cream cones for all!"; on another Sunday, plant flowers in containers to brighten your windowsill or front steps, and perhaps give some potted flowers as gifts. Take time to celebrate the new life of Christ in the midst of springtime.

Conversation Starter

What did Jesus say or do in the Gospel of this Sunday? Imagine, for a moment, that you are there in the Gospel. You are listening very closely and watching very closely. What do you see and hear? How do you feel?

Today's Prayer

Lord Jesus, every week we celebrate your Resurrection when we gather for the Eucharist. During this Easter season, help us to remember that you are alive and with us always, each and every moment!
Amen. Alleluia!

May

May baskets and Maypoles witness to the joy we feel when May finally makes an appearance. These customs originated in the somewhat milder climate of England. Sometimes May can be deceptively cool in much of the United States. It's not quite summer yet!

We welcome May nevertheless. After all, as an old hymn sings,
"'Tis the month of our Mother,
The blessed and beautiful May."

May *is* blessed and beautiful, and somehow we ourselves feel blessed and beautiful as the days grow warmer. The flower for May is the humble and fragrant Lily-of-the-Valley. This flower is legendarily known as "Our Lady's Tears," shed during the crucifixion of Jesus. As May is the month of Our Lady, this designated flower of May symbolizes her love and compassion!

 ## The Ascension of the Lord (Thursday of the Sixth Week of Easter or the Seventh Sunday of Easter)

Introduction
We celebrate the Ascension of the Lord forty days after Easter (or, the following Sunday in many dioceses). The Ascension is the final act of redemption that began on Good Friday. Jesus, as the Son of God, assumes his rightful place, sitting, as we proclaim in the Nicene Creed, "at the right hand of the Father."

Today's Reading
Go to www.usccb.org/bible/readings for the text or an audio recording of the Scripture readings for Thursday of the Sixth Week of Easter or the Seventh Sunday of Easter (the Ascension of the Lord).

Faith-Sharing Activity
It is natural for us to think of Heaven as "up." In today's Gospel, the angels are impatient with the Apostles because they are standing around, looking up, when they could be getting the mission started! However, today is a day to celebrate our ultimate destiny with Jesus. We, too, will ascend! Rather than celebrate with balloons (which harm the environment and choke animals or fish when swallowed), blow bubbles instead. You can find large wands to make giant bubbles. Bubbles reflect the light, which is a beautiful example of our lives as Christians: We want to reflect the Light of Jesus.

Conversation Starter

If we follow Jesus on earth, we will also follow him into Heaven. How does that make you feel? How are you following Jesus on earth?

Today's Prayer

Today we begin a novena (nine days of prayer) for the coming of the Holy Spirit. We can pray each day, "Come Holy Spirit, and fill our hearts with your love. Amen."

 ## Pentecost Sunday

Introduction

Pentecost Sunday is celebrated fifty days after Easter. It has its origins in a Jewish festival celebrated fifty days after Passover. Called the Feast of Weeks, it celebrated the giving of the Law on Mount Sinai. The Holy Spirit is the New Law, fulfilling the Old Law and written on our hearts.

Today's Reading

Go to www.usccb.org/bible/readings for the text or an audio recording of the Scripture readings for Pentecost Sunday.

Faith-Sharing Activity

Pentecost is sometimes called the birthday of the Church because it is the day the work of the Church began. Celebrate with a party! The color of the Holy Spirit is red (for the tongues of fire), so decorate with the colors of red and pink. Make ribbon wands to catch the wind (also a symbol of the Holy Spirit). Gather rulers, dowels, or even short branches, and tie or tape a few 24" red and pink ribbons to the ends. Choose some favorite music and allow sufficient space for swooping and swirling!

For a party, ice cream and cake seem appropriate. Red Velvet Cake comes to mind. Or, cakes or cupcakes with a plain white frosting can be decorated with candy hearts, because the Holy Spirit comes into our hearts to help us to follow Jesus.

Conversation Starter

The Holy Spirit gives us ideas for doing good things. What good things have you done lately? The Holy Spirit is at work in you!

Today's Prayer

Thank you, Holy Spirit, for coming to us and giving us ideas for doing good. Thank you for helping us to follow Jesus and to bring peace and love to the world. Amen.

May Crowning

Introduction

The crowning of a statue of the Blessed Mother has been a traditional parish devotion for many years. Usually an outdoor procession is held, with hymns sung in honor of Our Lady and the praying of the Litany of Loreto, which honors all the titles of Our Lady. The procession ends in church with the crowning.

Today's Reading

The May crowning is not part of the Church's official liturgy. An appropriate Scripture reading can be found in the Book of Revelation 12:1–6.

Faith-Sharing Activity

Setting up a home May altar is a beautiful way to honor Mary in her month of May. It is as easy as placing a statue or icon of Our Lady on a special table, and setting a vase of May flowers in front of or next to it. More elaborate decorations could include a wooden lattice or a bulletin board propped behind the altar, with blue and white crêpe paper chains twisted and tacked to form a backdrop. You may even want to have your own May crowning!

The May altar is an appropriate focal point for family prayer during May. You might try to pray together one decade of the Rosary (one Our Father and ten Hail Marys) before bedtime each night. See pages 103-104 for steps for praying the Rosary.

Conversation Starter

Mary is Jesus' Mother, and our Mother too. She wants to know what is happening in our lives. When will you talk to Mary? What do you think you will tell her?

Today's Prayer

Holy Mary, Mother of God, pray for us sinners, now and at the hour of our death. Amen.

SUMMER

Send us good summer, O Lord.
Winters have chilled us and stilled us too long.
Give us hearts on fire.
Be our true desire.
Send us your Spirit, O Lord.

(Dan Schutte, Oregon Catholic Press,
Here I Am, Lord, 30th Anniversary Edition)

June

Although the official first day of summer does not arrive until June 21, the change of season seems to begin when the school schedule ends and the summer schedule begins. Even though adult schedules do not change so abruptly, the milder weather and longer summer evenings seem to lure us into a more relaxed mode of being.

June is also a popular month for family events like graduations and weddings. Use them as "teaching moments": Talk about the importance of getting an education, discovering talents and following them, choosing an appropriate spouse. These values need to be articulated. Otherwise, life lessons are learned from watching television, flipping through online videos, or dubious advice from peers.

This month's flower, the rose, seems made for this month. Whether huge and elegant, singly or in a bouquet, or tumbling wildly over fences and trellises, this ubiquitous flower always adds a note of grace to any environment. The rose seems to know its own beautiful value and never loses its elegant self-confidence. The rose is a symbol of love, and as such reminds us that we were made in God's image and likeness. We, too, are beautiful in God's eyes. We are of ultimate and eternal value. We are loved.

Solemnity of the Most Sacred Heart of Jesus
(Nineteen Days after Pentecost Sunday)

Introduction
The Feast of the Sacred Heart celebrates Christ's love for all of humanity. The popularity of the feast increased through the apparitions of Jesus to Saint Margaret Mary Alacoque in seventeenth-century France.

Today's Reading
Go to www.usccb.org/bible/readings for the text or an audio recording of the Scripture readings for the Solemnity of the Sacred Heart.

Faith-Sharing Activity
The Gospel for today recounts Christ's suffering on the Cross, and the piercing of his side with a lance. On the Cross, Christ gave his life to us. As a reminder of his self-giving love, we place crucifixes in our homes. On this feast, you might want to cut small hearts from red paper, and, with your family, tape or tie a heart to each crucifix in your home as a reminder of the love of Christ that cost so much.

If you do not have a crucifix, cut a cross from cardboard, color it with brown marker or cover it with brown paper, and place a red paper heart in the center where Christ's body would be. You may want to write, "I love you this much," on the heart. Display this cross on a wall near your prayer table.

Conversation Starter
There is still suffering in the world. Jesus did not get rid of it, but he helps us get through it. How can we help people we know who are suffering? How can we help people whom we do not know?

Today's Prayer
Lord, as we look upon your cross, we ask you to look down upon us. Give us faith, hope, and love. We are sorry for what we have done wrong, and we will do better. Fill us with your love, and help us to share it with others.
Amen.

 The Sundays in Ordinary Time

Introduction
Ordinary Time takes its name from the Sundays that are numbered with ordinal numbers (1, 2, 3, etc.). This is the second period of Ordinary Time in the Church calendar. The first period comes between the Season of Christmas and the Season of Lent.

Today's Reading
Go to www.usccb.org/bible/readings for the text or an audio recording of the Scripture readings for each Sunday in Ordinary Time.

Faith-Sharing Activity
During Ordinary Time, the Church dwells more deeply on the life of Christ and the teachings of Christ. As a family, keep a journal of memorable Scripture quotations. Begin with an ordinary spiral notebook. Paste a plain white piece of paper on the cover and label it, "Our Family Scripture Notebook." Each week, after Mass, review the Scripture readings. Decide which quotations should be written down in the notebook. You might like to choose one or two from each reading, or a quote from the psalm. Then challenge family members to memorize a few words from one of the verses and recall it often during the week. It does not have to be the whole verse. Keeping the Word of God in our minds helps that Word to gradually penetrate our hearts.

Conversation Starter

What did Jesus do or say this Sunday? How can we live these words in our own lives? What verses can we choose to write in our family notebook? What words will we keep in mind this week?

Today's Prayer

Your words, O Lord, are light to our path. Lead us in the ways of peace. Amen.

Solemnity of the Nativity of Saint John the Baptist (June 24)

Introduction

When the feast of Christmas was established, the date of the birth of John the Baptist was assigned to June 24, as he was six months older than Jesus.

Today's Reading

Go to www.usccb.org/bible/readings for the text or an audio recording of the Scripture readings for the Nativity of Saint John the Baptist.

Faith-Sharing Activity

Saint John's Day comes near the first day of summer and has been traditionally celebrated with the lighting of bonfires, symbolizing the light of the sun. If possible, gather around a bonfire this evening. Play games ("I spy with my little eye something that begins with….") and make s'mores. Or, light a single candle and gather around it. Play "I spy" and share a special treat. End the evening with a prayer, asking Saint John's intercession for a blessed summer.

To play I Spy: The person who guesses the object correctly is the next to say "I spy." Questions can be asked, answered with yes or no, or "hot" (for close) or "cold" (for not close). The Spy can offer extra clues if the players are stumped.

Conversation Starter

Jesus and John may have played together as boys because they were cousins. Who do we spend our free time with? How should we treat the boys and girls we play with? How do we solve problems if they come up?

Today's Prayer

Lord Jesus, your cousin John announced you to the world. Help us announce you to our world by our words of kindness and our good actions. We ask in your name, Lord Jesus. Amen.

Solemnity of Saints Peter and Paul, Apostles (June 29)

Introduction

Saint Peter was the leader of the Apostles and the first Pope; Saint Paul brought the Good News to the Gentiles. Both died as martyrs and are known as "the pillars of the Church."

Today's Reading

Go to www.usccb.org/bible/readings for the text or an audio recording of the Scripture readings for the Solemnity of Saints Peter and Paul.

Faith-Sharing Activity

Celebrate this feast of the two pillars of the Church by proposing a challenge: "Two Is Better Than One." While driving or walking together, how many "two's" do you see? A "two" can be on a sign ("2-hour parking"). It can be someone walking two dogs. It can be two people walking together, or a two-seat stroller. If you like, keep track on paper, as individuals or teams.

At home, make a two-sided bookmark. Cut out two pieces of sturdy paper (2" x 6"). On one, write, "Saint Peter, pray for us." On the other write, "Saint Paul, pray for us." Glue the two pieces together so that the prayers can be read. Make a hole in the top. Take an 8" length of yarn, bend it in half, and put the loop through the hole. Push the ends of the yarn through that loop and pull.

Conversation Starter

Jesus called Peter a "rock" because his faith was strong. How is your faith like a rock? What would help your faith to grow and to become stronger?

Today's Prayer

Saints Peter and Paul, pray for us. Strengthen our faith in Christ, and help us to proclaim it in our words and actions.
Amen.

July

July begins with a bang! Summer is in full swing, and with it comes the birthday of the United States of America, celebrated every year on July 4.

The Church calendar gives us two important saints to celebrate this month: Saint Benedict on July 11 and Saint Mary Magdalene on July 22. Each of them was a lover of Christ, and made him known and loved throughout the world.

This month's flower is the larkspur or delphinium. This flower may be pink, white, or purple. One noteworthy characteristic of this plant is that it self-seeds. Without moving from its place, it re-seeds itself and thus comes back year after year. It does not like to be transplanted. It is happy where it is! Rooted in its own place, it yet spreads far and wide.

How true this is of the Benedictine Order and its offshoots, founded by Saint Benedict. From his monastery in Italy, the disciples of Benedict have spread far and wide, bringing the Gospel to the entire world, monastery by monastery. Each monastery is rooted to its own spot, yet continually throws out the seeds of Good News to all.

Saint Mary Magdalene, too, was only one person, one follower of Christ, but she became "the apostle to the Apostles" by witnessing to the Resurrection.

Memorial of Saint Benedict, Abbot
(July 11)

Introduction
Saint Benedict wrote what he called "a little rule for monks," and it became the foundation for most monastic communities in the West. Thus Benedict became known as "the founder of Western monasticism."

Today's Reading
Go to www.usccb.org/bible/readings for the text or an audio recording of the Scripture readings for the Memorial of Saint Benedict.

Faith-Sharing Activity
Make a cardboard Saint Benedict's medal for each member of the family. Trace a circle (using a large jar cover) on light cardboard and cut it out. Paste another circle, cut out from yellow paper, on the cardboard. On each circle, draw in pencil a Saint Benedict's cross: The arms are of even lengths stemming from the middle, and are slightly wider, or flared, at the circle end. Color the cross red. Punch two holes on either side of one of the arms of the cross. Insert string or ribbon into the holes so that the medal can be hung around the neck. Knot the ribbon on the backside of the medal. You may also write, "Saint Benedict, pray for our family" on the back of the medal. (Examples of Saint Benedict's medal can be found online.)

Conversation Starter

Saint Benedict wanted his monks to live like a loving family. What rules in your family help you to live together lovingly and peacefully? One of Benedict's rules was "Never let the sun go down on your anger." Why is that a good rule?

Today's Prayer

Saint Benedict, teach us to live in love, peace, and forgiveness of one another. Amen.

Memorial of Saint Mary Magdalene (July 22)

Introduction

The Gospel of today recounts the meeting of Mary Magdalene and the Risen Jesus in the garden. She does not recognize Jesus—until he speaks her name. Jesus knows us by name, too.

Today's Reading

Go to www.usccb.org/bible/readings for the text or an audio recording of the Scripture readings for the Memorial of Saint Mary Magdalene.

Faith-Sharing Activity

Celebrate baptismal names by making name placards. Using white drawing paper or printer paper (8½ inches x 11 inches), cut each piece in half lengthwise. Ask each family member to write his or her baptismal name on the half. (Little ones can have their names written for them.) Decorate with crayons and markers. On the back of each placard, write this verse from the prophet Isaiah: "I have called you by name; you are mine" (Isaiah 43:1).

Then take a small rectangle of cardboard (about 1½ inches x 5 inches) and bend it in two places, so that it is evenly divided into three sections. Place this behind the placard, at the bottom, and staple the placard to the middle section. This will allow the placard to stand up. Use the placards as "place cards" at your table this week.

Conversation Starter

What does it feel like to be called by name by Mom? By Dad? By a teacher? By a friend? How does it feel to know that Jesus calls you by name?

Today's Prayer

Lord Jesus, you call us by name as you called Mary's name in the garden. Help us to know you, to recognize you, and to share your love with all.

August

August takes its nickname, "the dog days of summer" from the "dog-star" (Sirius), the brightest star in the constellation *Canis Major* (Large Dog).

These hot summer days are punctuated by the Solemnity of the Assumption of Mary, or, as the Eastern Churches name the feast, the Dormition (or "falling asleep") of the *Theotokos* (God-bearer). In the Eastern Churches, this feast is preceded by a two-week fast. This custom has been taken on by Pax Christi, the Catholic organization dedicated to peace in the world, as a prayer for peace.

The Solemnity of the Assumption is a holy day of obligation. These holy days are not easy to celebrate in our culture. At one point in history, the entire culture observed Church festivals. But in our day, the secular world does not stop because we are observing a holy day. And, in some places, schools convene in August!

However, even if you work outside the home, you may be able to plan a vacation day on August 15. An old folk custom associates this feast with water. You might want to plan to participate in the feast-day Mass (or the vigil Mass) with your family, then spend the rest of the day at the shore, at the lake, or at your local swimming pool. Planning a family outing on this great Marian feast day is a wonderful way to honor the Mother of the Lord, Queen of Heaven and Earth.

This month's flower is the gladiolus, those tall, bright plants with the sword-shaped leaves, and flowers spiking from one side. In the Scriptures, the word of God is compared to a sword (see Hebrews 4:12 and Ephesians 6:17). Carry it with you into August!

Solemnity of the Assumption of the Blessed Virgin Mary (August 15)

Introduction
The feast celebrates the dormition (or "falling asleep") of Mary and her bodily assumption into Heaven, before her body could begin to decay. This feast foretells our own bodily resurrection, and has been celebrated since the sixth century.

Today's Reading
Go to www.usccb.org/bible/readings for the text or an audio recording of the Scripture readings for the Assumption of the Blessed Virgin Mary.

Faith-Sharing Activity

In many countries, this feast is the day on which people pray for a good harvest, and fruits and herbs are brought to church to be blessed and shared. A Portuguese custom that has found a home in the United States is the blessing of fishing boats and other watercraft on this feast day.

Today would be a good day to do some water play. At the kitchen sink, or in bins in the backyard, bring out washable dolls, doll clothes, plastic building blocks, toy vehicles, and other toys. Allow the children to give them a good washing and let them dry in the sun. You may also want to wash bikes or other outdoor equipment.

Use the hose or a sprinkler in other water activities if weather permits. If school is already in session, make time next weekend for some end-of-summer water play.

Conversation Starter

In the feast-day Gospel, Mary visited Elizabeth. What would you say to Mary if she visited you? What do you think Mary would say to you?

Today's Prayer

Mary, we honor you as Mother of God and our Mother, too. Keep us close to Jesus. Amen.

(You may want to pray a Hail Mary together.)

Memorial of Saint Augustine, Bishop and Doctor of the Church (August 28)

Introduction

Augustine was a catechumen (candidate for Baptism) for several years, because he did not want to give up his way of life and his wrong ways of thinking. His sainthood gives us hope!

Today's Reading

Go to www.usccb.org/bible/readings for the text or an audio recording of the Scripture readings for the Memorial of Saint Augustine.

Faith-Sharing Activity

Augustine's conversion came about while he was sitting under a fig tree in his garden. He heard a child chanting, "Take up and read! Take up and read!" Augustine opened the Scriptures, and they spoke to his heart. The natural world can inspire us to be open to God's message. Take a walk with your family in a nearby park or garden. Or, if you live near an ocean or lake, walk along the shore. What do you see and hear that reminds you of God? At home, make a mobile of the nature scene you experienced. Draw each part separately (a tree, a cloud, a pond) on white drawing paper, and attach them to a clothes hanger by varying lengths of string. On the back of one of your drawings, write "Saint Augustine, pray for us."

Conversation Starter

Augustine's mother was a saint, too. Her name is Monica. She prayed for Augustine all of his life. Why is it important to pray for others? Who should we pray for today?

Today's Prayer

Lord Jesus, thank you for bringing Saint Augustine to you, no matter how long it took. Thank you for your patience with us. Help us to turn to you always.
Amen.

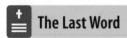 **The Last Word**

There is an appointed time for everything
    and a time for every affair under the heavens.
A time to give birth, and a time to die;
    a time to plant, and a time to uproot the plant.
A time to kill, and a time to heal;
    a time to tear down, and a time to build.
A time to weep, and a time to laugh;
    a time to mourn, and a time to dance.
A time to scatter stones, and a time to gather them;
    a time to embrace, and a time to be far from embraces.
A time to seek, and a time to lose;
    a time to keep, and a time to cast away.
A time to rend, and a time to sew;
    a time to be silent, and a time to speak.
A time to love, and a time to hate;
    a time of war, and a time of peace.

(Ecclesiastes 3:1–8)

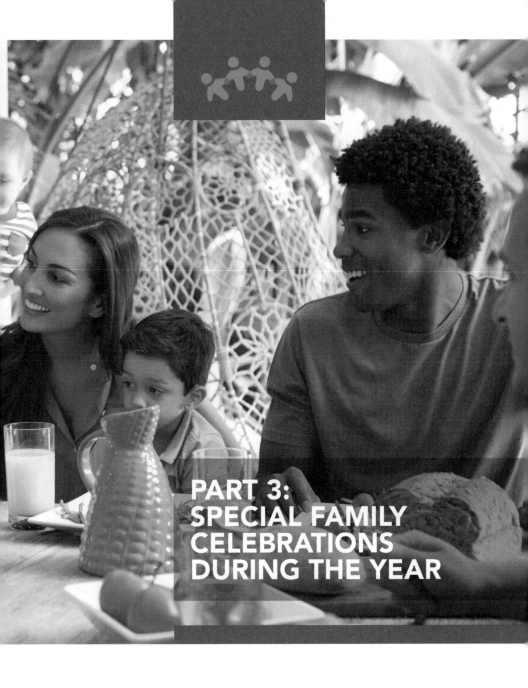

PART 3:
SPECIAL FAMILY
CELEBRATIONS
DURING THE YEAR

Being a disciple means being constantly ready to bring the love of Jesus to others, and this can happen unexpectedly and in any place: on the street, in a city square, during work, on a journey.

(Pope Francis, The Joy of the Gospel, #127)

There are other special days throughout the year that do not appear on the Church calendar. Still because these days are important for both family and society, they also provide an opportunity to show how they can be days of grace and of sharing the Gospel at home and with those we meet.

Grandparents' Day
(First Sunday after Labor Day)

Introduction

National Grandparents' Day was begun in 1978 through the hard work of Marian McQuade of Oak Hill, West Virginia. She wanted to educate youth about the important contributions of seniors, and to encourage families to visit the elderly and, if possible, to "adopt" a grandparent, not just for the day, but for a lifetime.

Today's Reading

Because Grandparents' Day is a secular holiday, no liturgical readings are given. However, you may want to look at July 26, the feast of Saints Joachim and Anne, the parents of Mary and the grandparents of Jesus. Go to www.usccb.org/bible/readings for the text or an audio recording of the Scripture readings for July 26, the Memorial of Saints Joachim and Anne.

Faith-Sharing Activity

If Grandparents' Day is observed as a school event, you may want to participate. If grandparents live elsewhere, you may want to invite a kindly neighbor or other familiar senior adult to visit your child's school. (You may want to phone or videoconference the far-away grandparents as well.)

It is also important to remember those living in retirement centers or assisted living facilities. Gather paper and crayons, and, as a family, make and decorate several cards that say, "Happy Grandparents' Day!" Drop them off at a nearby retirement center and ask that they be distributed to those residents who may not receive many visitors. Sign your names as "The _____ Family."

Conversation Starter

Why is it so nice to have grandparents? What can we do that would be nice for Nana and Gramps [use your family words]?

Today's Prayer

O God, our Father, you have given us grandparents. . We are grateful for all that they do for us. Keep them in your care. We pray for all grandparents who have died. May they continue to watch over their families from the center of your love.
Amen.

Halloween
(All Hallows' Eve, October 31)

Introduction

The word Halloween means "All Hallows' Eve," because the day is the eve of All Saints' Day. Contrary to some current opinions, Halloween is not a day to celebrate evil and darkness; rather, it's a day to rejoice in Christ's victory over sin and death. Traditionally, Halloween was a day of fasting before celebrating the Feast of All Saints on November 1. The practice of going door to door, begging for treats, originated in the Middle Ages.

Today's Reading

There are no official readings for Halloween, as it is the vigil of All Saints' Day. Instead, you may go to www.usccb.org/bible/readings for the text or an audio recording of the Scripture readings for the day.

Faith-Sharing Activity

It is the custom in some places to have a Halloween costume parade, with the children dressed as their patron saint or favorite saint. This is a wonderful way to underline the connection between Halloween and All Saints' Day.

As you carve pumpkins and plan costumes, talk about the real meaning of Halloween—a time when we think about death, about ghosts and skeletons, but in a way that emphasizes Christ's power over it. We don't have to be afraid of death, because Christ has already won the victory over it ("Where, O death, is your victory? Where, O death, is your sting?" asked Saint Paul [1 Corinthians 15:55]).

Conversation Starter

Human beings have always wondered what happens at death, and afterwards. Halloween is a good opportunity to answer the question "What happens when we die?" *(At death, the life of our bodies, the soul, leaves and goes to live with God. Through Jesus, we have new life forever with God!)*

Today's Prayer

Risen Lord Jesus, thank you for conquering death by your own death and Resurrection. As we celebrate Halloween, and enjoy our parties, trick-or-treating, and costumes, help us to remember that you gave us true joy by your victory of life over death. Give us that life forever!
Amen.

Thanksgiving Day
(The Fourth Thursday in November)

Introduction
The instinct to be grateful lies deep in every honest human heart, and the Puritan emigrants to these shores in the seventeenth century had every reason to thank God for their survival. Although celebrated on various days throughout the history of our country, President Franklin D. Roosevelt officially fixed the Thanksgiving holiday on the fourth Thursday of November.

Today's Reading
Go to www.usccb.org/bible/readings for the text or an audio recording of the Scripture readings for Thanksgiving Day.

Faith-Sharing Activity
The word *Eucharist* means "thanksgiving." Celebrate your gratitude to God this day by celebrating the Eucharist with your parish family. Special Mass readings and prayers link our faith with this traditional American holiday.

As a family, compose a special Thanksgiving grace before meals. Mention blessings experienced by your family in the past year.

It is a custom in some families to give each family member and guest at the table an opportunity to mention a blessing gratefully received in the past year.

Participate in Thanksgiving food drives or winter coat collections. Show gratitude by giving.

Conversation Starter
Why is an "attitude of gratitude" important not only on Thanksgiving Day but in everyday life?

Today's Prayer
Pray this traditional grace after meals to end your Thanksgiving meal:

We give you thanks, almighty God, for these and all your blessings, which we have received through Christ, our Lord.
Amen.

Valentine's Day
(February 14)

Introduction

Saint Valentine is no longer commemorated in the general Church calendar because so little is known about him. He is still listed in the Roman Martyrology. Imprisoned for his faith, he wrote encouraging letters to the Christian community.

Today's Reading

An appropriate reading for Valentine's Day is Saint Paul's instruction on the meaning of love. See 1 Corinthians 13:1–13.

Faith-Sharing Activity

Valentine's Day is a day to celebrate Christian friendship. Encourage your children to send valentines not only to their best friends but also to those children who may not have many friends. "You can't judge a book by its cover," and sometimes finding a diamond in the rough takes a little digging!

Gather your family to make Scripture valentines. You will need small paper doilies and red construction paper. Make a pattern by drawing a heart on a piece of cardboard. Cut it out and trace it on the red paper. Make two red hearts for each doily, pasting one on the front and one on the back.

On the back heart, write one of the phrases from Saint Paul's Letter to the Corinthians, noted above. Distribute the Scripture valentines to family members, friends, and those who might appreciate these messages.

Conversation Starter

"Love is a verb"—not a feeling, but an action. What loving actions can we do for others today?

Today's Prayer

Lord Jesus, may the words we speak and write encourage others, as did the letters and loving notes of Saint Valentine.
Amen.

Mother's Day
(The Second Sunday in May)

Introduction

The accounts of the origins of this day vary, but it is interesting to note that Andrews' Methodist Episcopal Church in Grafton, West Virginia, has become the International Mother's Day Shrine. The church building has been designated a National Historic Landmark.

Today's Reading

Mother's Day is not a liturgical feast, but an appropriate reading for this day would be Ben Sira (Sirach) 3:1–16.

Faith-Sharing Activity

On this day set aside to honor mothers, we invite all the moms in the family to sit back and relax! It is good to remember that not all mothers have given birth in a physical way. Today is a good day to remember godmothers at Baptism and Confirmation, stepmothers, aunts, and good friends who have been mothers to us spiritually. If you have been blessed with a spiritual mother, be sure to send a card or make a phone call to connect with that special person today.

There may be mothers and grandmothers in assisted living and retirement centers who also would appreciate your attention, whether they are related to you or not. You might prepare some special cards to bring to a nearby retirement facility. Ask that the cards be distributed to those who did not receive a Mother's Day card from their own family.

Conversation Starter

God's commandment says, "Honor your father and your mother." How do you honor your mother, not only on Mother's Day, but every day?

Today's Prayer

Mother Mary, you know the joys and sorrows of all mothers. As we celebrate Mother's Day, help us to show our own mother the love and respect she deserves. Amen.

Memorial Day
(Last Monday In May)

> ## Introduction
> *Formerly known as Decoration Day, May 30 was set aside after the Civil War as a day to honor all those who had died in that war. In 1971, the observance was moved to the last Monday in May. Now it is a day to honor all those who died in all of our nation's wars.*

Today's Reading
Today is not a liturgical feast day, but an appropriate reading for this day would be Wisdom 3:1–9.

Faith-Sharing Activity
The poppy is the symbol of Memorial Day, inspired by the poem, "In Flanders' Fields," written after World War I. All during May, you may find artificial poppies being offered by veterans' groups in exchange for a donation.

Picnics and parades are also popular and appropriate. The original purpose of Memorial Day was to decorate the graves of fallen soldiers, so many families visit cemeteries and plant flowers on family graves. American flags are placed on the graves of veterans.

In the year 2000, a congressional resolution was passed, asking that, at 3 p.m. on this day, all Americans might observe a moment of remembrance and respect during a moment of silence, during which "Taps" might be played.

Participating in these events reminds us that war has a cost, and, as the *Catechism of the Catholic Church* reminds us, it should only be entered into as a last resort.

Conversation Starter
Who are the veterans in our family, both living and deceased, who have served our country? (Mention also volunteers for the Peace Corps, Teach for America, and other organizations.) How can we thank them today?

Today's Prayer
Let us pray the last three lines of "Taps" for our deceased veterans:

"All is well. Safely rest. God is nigh." We commend them into your hands, O God. Amen.

The Last Day of School

Introduction

Today is a day of celebration for both students and teachers. Day in and day out, they have made their way toward the finish line together and, today, they have made it! Whatever the summer may bring, they are ready for it!

As a family, complete all of the following faith-sharing steps, or do one or more as your time permits.

Today's Reading
This reading from the Old Testament hints at the value of a good education: Ben Sira (Sirach) 8:8–9.

Faith-Sharing Activity
It is the custom in some areas to have a child bring a gift to the teacher on the last day of school. If your child's experience has been a good one, perhaps the best gift would be a personal note from your child thanking his or her teacher for a year of growth and accomplishment. A few examples of a good experience in the classroom could be mentioned in the note. Some teachers keep such notes from students in a special box and treasure them for the rest of their lives. Teaching is a very important job, but it is not easy. We say "thank you" to people who help us, and we should certainly thank those who help us grow and learn. As a familiar bumper sticker reminds us, "If you can read this, thank a teacher!"

Conversation Starter
The reading from Ben Sira (above) encourages us to listen to our elders. Which elders do you listen to? Can you remember something that you have learned from your elders?

Today's Prayer
Thank you, Lord, for this school year. Help us to keep learning during the summer, so that both our brains and our bodies will get exercise in the days ahead.
Amen.

Father's Day
(The Third Sunday in June)

Introduction

When Jesus prayed the Our Father, he used the word Abba. *This is the familiar word for* father *in Aramaic. It could be translated, "Daddy." How close God wants to be to us!*

Father's Day was signed into law as an official American holiday in 1972.

Today's Reading

Father's Day is not celebrated on the Church calendar, but an appropriate reading for this day might be Ben Sira (Sirach) 3:1–6 and 12–16.

Faith-Sharing Activity

This is a day to fuss over Dad—in simple, homemade ways. A pointed golden crown can be made from yellow construction paper. Draw lightly lengthwise on the paper. Cut out and staple the ends together. Staple an extra paper band to lengthen it at the back if needed. Or, cut out a circle from cardboard (a jar lid can be used as a guide) and cover it with white paper. Tape two inch-wide blue or gold ribbons to it underneath. Print on the circle, "#1 Dad." Present the ribbon to Dad with his favorite meal and a present. A homemade card and an "action gift" noted inside (something the card-maker will do for Dad in the near future) is also an appropriate way to honor a father.

Conversation Starter

Today we honor dads and those who are "like fathers" to us (coaches, Scout leaders, etc.). How do they help us in our lives? How can we honor these men today and every day?

Today's Prayer

God our Father, thank you for our dad. Help him in all he is and does for us. Amen.

Independence Day
(Founding of the United States of America, July 4)

Introduction
Today we celebrate the founding of the United States of America. On this date in 1776, representatives from all thirteen of the former British colonies adopted the Declaration of Independence.

Today's Reading
For the optional proper Mass for Independence Day, choose among the readings used at Mass for this celebration: Isaiah 32:15–18, Psalm 85, and Matthew 5:1–12a.

Faith-Sharing Activity
Our country and its leaders need our prayers. For one week, from July 4 through July 10, include a prayer for our country in your family table grace or other prayers. Cut out seven stars from red, white, and blue construction paper. On each star, write the name of one government official to pray for. These names might include the President of the United States, your two senators, your congressperson, or your mayor or other local official. Scramble the stars. Each day, pick one star and pray for that person, that he or she may make the decisions that will be most helpful to our country and its citizens. You might use the prayer below, or make up one of your own.

Conversation Starter
How can we love and care for our country? How can we be helpful to other countries in our world? Why is it important to vote in elections in our country?

Today's Prayer
"My country, right or wrong; if right, to be *kept* right; and if wrong, to be *set* right" (Carl Schurz, Senator and Union Army general in the Civil War). Help us, God, to do our part.
Amen.

PART 4: PRAYERS AND BLESSINGS THROUGHOUT THE YEAR

Have no anxiety at all, but in everything by prayer and petition, with thanksgiving, make your requests known to God. Then the peace of God that surpasses all understanding will guard your hearts and minds in Christ Jesus.

(Philippians 4:6–7)

Family Prayer

A slogan made popular by Father Patrick Peyton, CSC, a Holy Cross priest, says very succinctly, "The family that prays together stays together." He meant the slogan to encourage families of the 1950s to adopt the family Rosary as a nightly practice, but we can expand the idea to all prayer at all times!

Prayer should be as natural to us as breathing. In fact, the Hebrew word for *spirit* (and the Holy Spirit is the source of all our prayer) is *ruah*, or "breath." We cannot see our breath, but it keeps us alive. Without being able to breathe, our body shuts down and we die.

We cannot see prayer. Prayer is a mystery between God and the human person. But prayer is really what keeps us alive. Without prayer, our spirits will gradually shut down. We will die spiritually.

Children learn by doing. They learn by imitation. They want to do what mom and dad do. If mom and dad pray, they will learn to pray. Of course they should learn to speak to God in their own words, spontaneously. Parents can model this. But they should also learn the traditional prayers of the community: the Our Father, the Hail Mary, and the Glory to the Father. (See Part 5 for these and more.) Parents can also model these traditional prayers at various times: before and after meals, while beginning a car trip, before bed, and as opportunities present themselves during the day.

In this section, prayers are suggested for various occasions, both happy and sad. God knows how we feel. But when we place our thoughts and feelings in his hands, we give him permission to help us and to heal us. We no longer feel alone. In the presence of our loving Father, we can find peace.

 **Prayers for Happy Times**

"This is the day the LORD has made;
    let us rejoice in it and be glad."
(Psalm 118:24)

A Prayer of Welcome for a Newborn Child
"You formed my inmost being;
    you knit me in my mother's womb.
I praise you, because I am wonderfully made;
    wonderful are your works!"
(Psalm 139:13–14)

Thank you, God our Father, for our new baby. We welcome this gift of love from you. May we help this new baby grow by our love and care. We ask this in the name of Jesus, who once was a new baby himself. Amen.

A Prayer of Welcome for an Adopted Child

"In love he destined us for adoption to himself through Jesus Christ, in accord with the favor of his will, for the praise of the glory of his grace that he granted us in the beloved."
(Ephesians 1:5–6)

Thank you, God our Father, for our new child and the newest member of our family. We thank you for choosing this child to join our family. May we help *(her or him)* to grow, to develop the gifts and talents you have given to *(her or him)*, and to belong to one another always. We ask as your own adopted children, in the name of Jesus. Amen.

A Prayer on the Anniversary of Baptism

"The Spirit and the bride say, 'Come.' Let the hearer say, 'Come.' Let the one who thirsts come forward, and the one who wants it receive the gift of life-giving water."
(Revelation 22:17)

O God, Holy Trinity, we thank you today for the anniversary of Baptism of _____. As *(he or she)* was baptized in the name of the Father, and of the Son, and of the Holy Spirit, and was made your beloved child, help *(him or her)* to live the Christian life with faith, hope, love, and joy. We ask this in the name of Jesus. Amen.

A Prayer on the Anniversary of Marriage

"That is why a man leaves his father and mother and clings to his wife, and the two of them become one body." *(Genesis 2:24)*

Thank you, God, for bringing _____ and _____ *(us)* together in marriage. As we remember and celebrate the day of their *(our)* wedding vows, may we see them *(ourselves)* as a sign of your great love for all of your children. May they *(we)* live that love always. We ask this in the name of Jesus. Amen.

A Prayer on the Name Day of a Patron Saint

We give thanks "to the Father, who has made you fit to share in the inheritance of the holy ones in light."
(Colossians 1:12)

Dear God, thank you for giving me _____ as my name-day saint. Help me to learn more about *(him or her)*. As I celebrate this name day, may I always remember that I have a special friend in Heaven who wants to help me follow Jesus. In his name. Amen.

A Prayer on First Communion Day

"Then the two [disciples] recounted what had taken place on the way and how he [Jesus] was made known to them in the breaking of the bread."
(Luke 24:35)

Dear Jesus, thank you for coming to me for the very first time in the Eucharist. Help me remember that the Bread is really your Body and that the Cup holds your Blood, under the appearances of ordinary bread and wine. As you become part of me, may I become more like you. In your name, Lord Jesus. Amen.

A Prayer to Celebrate a Birthday

"Before I formed you in the womb I knew you, before you were born I dedicated you, a prophet to the nations I appointed you."
(Jeremiah 1:5)

Thank you, God, for creating me. You know it is my birthday! Thank you for making me unique in all the world. Thank you for giving me gifts and talents that I may not even know about yet. Thank you for my parents, relatives, and friends who help me grow. In the name of Jesus. Amen.

Prayers for Sad Times

"Lord, hear my prayer;
> let my cry come to you.
Do not hide your face from me
> in the day of my distress.
Turn your ear to me;
> when I call, answer me quickly."
(Psalm 102:1–3)

A Prayer When a Loved One Dies

"They seemed, in the view of the foolish, to be dead;
> *and their passing away was thought an affliction*
> *and their going forth from us, utter destruction.*
But they are in peace."
(Wisdom 3:2–3)

Dear God, we feel empty and alone because _____ has died. We believe that *(he or she)* is living with you. Take *(him or her)* to yourself, and give us the peace of knowing that *(he or she)* is still with us in a new way. May we all love one another in you. In the name of Jesus. Amen.

A Prayer for a Loved One Who Is Very Ill

"Though I am afflicted and poor,
My Lord keeps me in mind.
You are my help and deliverer;
My God, do not delay!"
(Psalm 40:18)

O God, _____ is facing a hard challenge. Be with *(him or her)* and strengthen *(him or her)* to know that *(she or he)* does not face this challenge alone. If it is your will, heal *(him or her)* of all illness and pain. To you be glory forever and ever. In the name of Jesus. Amen.

A Prayer for a Loved One Who Has Lost a Job

"Why are you downcast, my soul,
why do you groan within me?
Wait for God, for I shall again praise him,
my savior and my God."
(Psalm 42:12)

Lord Jesus, _____ has lost a job. Be with *(him or her)*. Remind all of us that we are not only "human doings" but also human beings. Show _____ the next right step to take in finding work, so that *(his or her)* gifts and talents will once more build up your Kingdom on earth. We ask in your name, Lord Jesus. Amen.

A Prayer after Receiving Bad News

"I heard a loud voice from the throne saying, 'Behold, God's dwelling is with the human race. He will dwell with them and they will be his people and God himself will always be with them [as their God]. He will wipe every tear from their eyes, and there shall be no more death or mourning, wailing or pain, [for] the old order has passed away.'"
(Revelation 21:3–4)

O God, we have just heard that _____. We are sad and upset. Be with us and show us how to support one another in this time of sorrow. We ask in the name of Jesus, your Son, who bore the Cross and rose again for us. Amen.

PART 5: TRADITIONAL PRAYERS AND DEVOTIONS

Sign of the Cross
In the name of the Father,
And of the Son,
And of the Holy Spirit.
Amen.

Lord's Prayer
Our Father, who art in heaven,
hallowed be thy name;
thy kingdom come;
thy will be done
on earth as it is in heaven.
Give us this day our daily bread;
and forgive us our trespasses
as we forgive those who trespass against us;
and lead us not into temptation,
but deliver us from evil.
Amen.

Hail Mary
Hail Mary, full of grace,
the Lord is with thee.
Blessed art thou among women,
and blessed is the fruit of thy womb, Jesus.
Holy Mary, Mother of God,
pray for us sinners,
now and at the hour of our death.
Amen.

Glory Be
Glory be to the Father,
and to the Son,
and to the Holy Spirit.
As it was in the beginning,
is now, and ever shall be,
world without end.
Amen.

Prayer to the Holy Spirit
Come, Holy Spirit, fill the hearts of your faithful,
and kindle in them the fire of your love.
Send forth your Spirit and they shall be created,
and you will renew the face of the earth.

Prayer to Jesus Christ in the Eucharist
Lord Jesus, I believe that you are truly present in the
Eucharist.

As I receive you in Holy Communion,
help me to love as you loved,
serve as you served,
so I can be the Body of Christ to others.
Amen.

The Apostles' Creed

I believe in God,
the Father almighty,
creator of heaven and earth,
and in Jesus Christ, his only Son, our Lord,
who was conceived by the Holy Spirit,
born of the Virgin Mary,
suffered under Pontius Pilate,
was crucified, died, and was buried;
he descended into hell;
on the third day he rose again from the dead;
he ascended into heaven,
and is seated at the right hand of God the Father almighty;
from there he will come to judge the living and the dead.

I believe in the Holy Spirit,
the holy catholic Church,
the communion of saints,
the forgiveness of sins,
the resurrection of the body,
and life everlasting.
Amen.

Hail Holy Queen

Hail, holy Queen, mother of mercy,
our life, our sweetness, and our hope!
To you we cry, poor banished children of Eve;
to you we send up our sighs,
mourning and weeping in this valley of tears.
Turn, then, most gracious advocate,
your eyes of mercy toward us;
and after this, our exile,
show unto us the blessed fruit of your womb, Jesus.
O clement, O loving, O sweet Virgin Mary!

The Angelus

Leader: The angel of the Lord declared unto Mary;
All: And she conceived by the Holy Spirit.
     Hail Mary…
Leader: Behold the handmaid of the Lord.
All: Be it done unto me according to your word.
     Hail Mary…
Leader: And the Word was made flesh,

All: And dwelt among us.
          Hail Mary…
Leader: Pray for us, O holy Mother of God,
All: That we may be made worthy of the promises of Christ.
Leader: Let us pray.
All: Pour forth, we beseech you, O Lord, your grace into our hearts, that we, to
          whom the incarnation of Christ, your Son, was made known by the mes-
          sage of an angel, may by his passion and Cross be brought the glory of his
          Resurrection, through the same Christ our Lord. Amen.

🌼 *Our Lady of Guadalupe Prayer*

Our Lady of Guadalupe,
Mystical Rose,
make intercession for the holy Church,
protect the Sovereign Pontiff,
help all those who invoke thee in their necessities,
and since thou art the ever Virgin Mary
and Mother of the true God,
obtain for us from thy most holy Son
the grace of keeping our faith,
sweet hope in the midst of the bitterness of life,
burning charity
and the precious gift of final perseverance.
Amen. *Saint Pius X*

🌼 *Prayer to the Divine Mercy*

God of everlasting mercy,
through the Eucharist you strengthen our faith.
kindle the faith of the people you have made your own,
increase, we pray, the grace you have bestowed,
that all may grasp and rightly understand
in what font they have been washed,
by whose Spirit they have been reborn,
by whose Blood they have been redeemed.
Through our Lord Jesus Christ, your Son,
who lives and reigns with you in the unity of the Holy Sprit,
one God, forever and ever. Amen.
Based on the Collect from Divine Mercy Sunday, *Roman Missal*

🌼 *Saint Joseph Prayer*

Saint Joseph, guardian of **Jesus** and chaste husband of **Mary**,
you passed your life in loving fulfillment of duty.
You supported the holy family of Nazareth with the work of your hands.
Kindly protect those who trustingly come to you.
You know their aspirations, their hardships, their hopes.
They look to you because they know you will understand and protect them.
You too knew trial, labor, and weariness.
But amid the worries of material life,
your soul was full of deep peace

and sang out in true joy through intimacy with God's Son entrusted to you,
and, with Mary, his tender Mother.
Assure those you protect that they do not labor alone.
Teach them to find Jesus near them and to watch over him faithfully as you
have done. Amen.
Saint John XXIII

 Peace Prayer of Saint Francis

Lord, make me an instrument of your peace.
Where there is hatred, let me sow love;
Where there is injury, pardon;
Where there is doubt, faith;
Where there is despair, hope;
Where there is darkness, light;
Where there is sadness, joy.

O divine Master, grant that I may not so much seek
To be consoled as to console,
To be understood as to understand,
To be loved as to love.
For it is in giving that we receive;
It is in pardoning that we are pardoned;
It is in dying that we are born to eternal life.

A Prayer for Families (World Meeting of Families Prayer)

God and Father of us all,
In Jesus, your Son and our Savior,
You have made us your sons and daughters
In the family of the Church.

May your grace and love help our families
In every part of the world
Be united to one another
In fidelity to the Gospel.

May the example of the Holy Family,
With the aid of your Holy Spirit,
Guide all families,
Especially those most troubled,
To be homes of communion and prayer
And to always seek your truth and live in your love.

Through Christ our Lord. Amen.

Jesus, Mary, and Joseph,
Pray for us!

Prayer before Meals

Bless us, O Lord, and these thy
gifts which we are about to
receive from thy bounty through
Christ our Lord.
Amen.

❀ *Prayer after Meals*

Father of mercy,
we praise you and give you glory
for the wonderful gifts you have given us:
for life and health, for faith and love,
and for this meal we have shared together.
Father, we thank you through Christ our Lord.
Amen.

❀ *Bedtime Prayer and Blessing*

Parent: May God bless you and keep you.
Child: May he guide you in life.
Parent: May he bless you this evening.
Child: And keep us in his sight.
Parent: May God be with you, *(child's name)*.
Child: And with your spirit.
Together, make the Sign of the Cross.

❀ *Vocation Prayer*

Lord, show me how to be of service in your Church and in the world.
Help me see what you want me to do.
Give me vision, courage, and friends
who encourage me to do your work. Amen.

❀ *Examination of Conscience for Children*

As you prepare to celebrate the Sacrament of Penance and Reconciliation, complete an examination of conscience. Reflect on each of the Ten Commandments. Think about how your words and actions have pleased God and how they might have offended him.

1. **I am the Lord your God, you shall not have other gods before me.** Do I always show my love for God? Do I always try to please him?
2. **You shall not take the name of the Lord, your God, in vain.** Do I always speak about God, Mary, and the saints with respect?
3. **Remember to keep holy the Sabbath.** Do I go to Mass every Sunday and on Holy Days of Obligation?
4. **Honor your father and mother.** Do I obey my parents and other adults who care for me? Do I listen to them with respect?
5. **You shall not kill.** Do I show respect for all human life? Do I treat others with kindness and love?
6. **You shall not commit adultery.** Do I treat my body and the bodies of others with respect?
7. **You shall not steal.** Have I taken anything that does not belong to me? Do I cheat or help others to cheat?
8. **You shall not bear false witness against your neighbor.** Do I always tell the truth, even when it is hard?
9. **You shall not covet your neighbor's wife.** Do I dress, talk, and act in a way that shows that I respect myself and others?
10. **You shall not covet your neighbor's goods.** Am I jealous of what others have? Do I wish that what others have belonged to me?

🏵 How to Go to Confession

Remember that you can celebrate the sacrament by speaking to the priest face to face or behind the screen.

1. **The priest welcomes you.** You tell him how long it has been since your last confession. You can use these words: "Bless me, Father, for I have sinned. It has been (number of weeks or months) since my last confession." The priest will lead you in making the Sign of the Cross.

2. **You listen to a Scripture reading.** The priest may read a short Scripture passage about God's love and mercy. Listen to the reading prayerfully.

3. **You confess your sins.** Think about the examination of conscience you completed. Tell the priest all the things that you have said or done that may have offended God. Do your best to tell all the sins you have committed. The priest will help you think about how you can avoid sin and please God. He will then give you a penance to complete. This may be a prayer and an act of kindness that you can do.

4. **You ask God for forgiveness.** You express sorrow for your sins and your love for God by praying an Act of Contrition.

5. **You receive absolution.** The priest extends his hands over your head. He says the prayer of absolution. He forgives your sins in the name of the Father, the Son, and the Holy Spirit.

6. **You say a prayer of thanksgiving.** The priest continues with these words: "Give thanks to the Lord, for he is good." You respond: "His mercy endures forever." After you leave the confessional, you take time to pray. If the priest asked you to pray a prayer for your penance, you pray it now. You thank God for his forgiveness. You promise God and yourself that you will try to please him.

🏵 Act of Contrition

My God, I am sorry for my sins with all my heart.
In choosing to do wrong and failing to do good,
I have sinned against you, whom I should love above all things.
I firmly intend, with your help, to do penance, to sin no more,
and to avoid whatever leads me to sin.
Our Savior Jesus Christ suffered and died for us.
In His name, my God, have mercy.
Amen.
Rite of Penance

🏵 The Rosary

The practice of praying the Rosary grew out of the monastic practice of praying the 150 psalms each week. Those who could not read the psalms were allowed to pray a Hail Mary for each one instead. These prayers were counted on beads, which have evolved into the five-decade chain of rosary beads that we use today. A decade is a set of ten Hail Marys, each decade separated by a larger bead for the Our Father. An event of Christ's life is attached to each decade under three traditional categories: the Joyful Mysteries, the Sorrowful Mysteries, and the Glorious mysteries. Together, these three sets make up the entire Rosary of 150 Hail Marys. Saint John Paul II added another set, the Mysteries of Light, to these three sets.

Begin the Rosary with the Sign of the Cross and the Apostles' Creed (prayed while holding the crucifix). Pray an Our Father on the large bead, a Hail Mary on each of the next three beads, and the Glory Be to the Father on the next large bead. Then begin the first decade of ten Hail Marys.

...ysteries (Monday and Saturday)

...e Annunciation

The Visitation

3. The Birth of Jesus
4. The Presentation of Jesus in the Temple
5. The Finding of Jesus in the Temple

Sorrowful Mysteries (Tuesday and Friday)

1. The Agony in the Garden
2. The Scourging at the Pillar
3. The Crowning with Thorns
4. The Carrying of the Cross
5. The Crucifixion

Glorious Mysteries (Wednesday and Sunday)

1. The Resurrection
2. The Ascension
3. The Coming of the Holy Spirit on the Apostles
4. The Assumption of Mary into Heaven
5. The Crowning of Mary as Queen of Heaven

Luminous Mysteries (Thursday)

1. The Baptism of Jesus
2. The Miracle at Cana
3. Jesus Proclaims the Kingdom of God
4. The Transfiguration of Jesus
5. The Institution of the Eucharist

The Stations of the Cross

Approach each station. Then announce the station. After a brief moment of reflection, pray the following:

Leader: We adore you, O Christ, and we praise you.
All: Because by your holy Cross, you have redeemed the world.

1. Jesus is condemned to death.
2. Jesus accepts the Cross.
3. Jesus falls the first time.
4. Jesus meets his Mother.
5. Simon helps Jesus carry the Cross.
6. Veronica wipes the face of Jesus.
7. Jesus falls the second time.
8. Jesus meets the women of Jerusalem.
9. Jesus falls the third time.
10. Jesus is stripped of his garments.
11. Jesus is nailed to the Cross.
12. Jesus dies on the Cross.
13. Jesus is taken down from the Cross.
14. Jesus is buried in the tomb.

You may also pray the 15th station facing the sanctuary or tabernacle in the church.

15. Jesus rises from the Dead.